TALKING POTS

Deciphering the Symbols of a
Prehistoric People

*A Study of the Prehistoric Pottery Icons
of the White Mountains of Arizona*

by

James R. Cunkle

GOLDEN
WEST ✦
PUBLISHERS

Photography by James R. Cunkle

Library of Congress Cataloging-in-Publication Data

Cunkle, James R.
  Talking Pots: Prehistoric Pottery Icons of the White Mountains of Arizona/by James R.Cunkle.
          p.   cm.
  Includes bibliographical references and index.
  1. Raven Site (Arizona.) 2. Pueblo Indians—Pottery. 3. Pottery, Prehistoric Arizona—
Raven Site—Themes, motives. 4. Mimbres culture—Arizona—Raven Site.
  5. Pueblo Indians—Antiquities.
  I. Title
E99.P9C847 1993   93-9843
979. 1 '37—dc20   CIP

3rd Printing ©1996

Printed in the United States of America

ISBN # 0-914846-81-7

Golden West Publishers
4113 N. Longview Ave.
Phoenix, AZ 85014, USA
(602) 265-4392

Dedication

To my father.
He would often show me entire worlds
by as simple an act
as turning a stone on the forest floor.

Acknowledgments

The first thank you that is due goes to the prehistoric craftswomen who created the icons on the ceramic vessels presented here. By painting the world they perceived around them and using the recognized symbols of their day, they inadvertently preserved for all time their legends and stories.

Thank you Ruth and Wendell Sherwood for all of your help over these many years of survey and excavation.

I would also like to thank Maria Lathum for her fine artwork and for putting up with my impossible deadlines.

A special thank you to my wife Carol who tolerated an army of dirty excavators in sleeping bags on her living room floor year after year.

Thank you Lee and Bruce for having the guts to gamble.

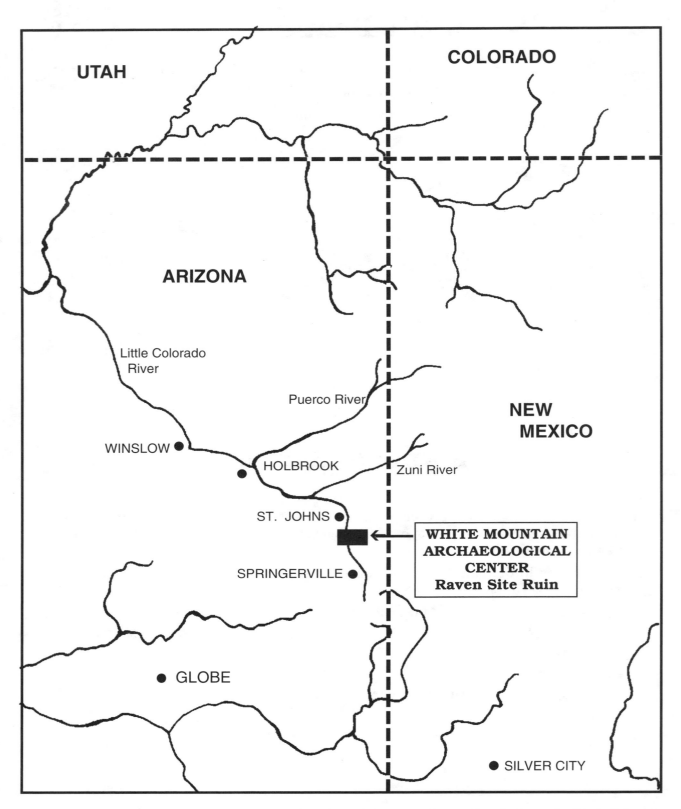

Figure 1. Location of the White Mountain Archaeological Center at Raven Site Ruin, on the Little Colorado Plateau at the northern edge of the White Mountains. This area lies in between the Anasazi cultural areas to the north and the Mogollon cultural areas to the south. Raven Site exhibits cultural material from both groups.

About the White Mountain Archaeological Center

The White Mountain Archaeological Center is a nonprofit facility and was initially established to protect and preserve Raven Site Ruin. It has evolved into far more. The Center now not only directs the excavation and curation of the cultural material from the site, including all of the ceramics included in this book, but also offers hands-on archaeological excavation, lab work and survey to anyone with an interest in the archaeological sciences. The Center is open from April through October. Daily, multiple day and week long programs are available. On-site lodging is available by reservation.

The on-site museum displays much of the cultural material discovered at Raven Site, and all of the artifacts are held in the repository at the same location. It is a rare opportunity to view all of the cultural material from a prehistoric pueblo in one place. Virtually all of the ceramic vessels illustrated in this book are on display at the Center, and they can be seen there seven days a week throughout the summer excavation season. Each year as the excavations continue, we eagerly await the cleaning and analysis in the lab, hoping that another Rosetta Stone similar to vessel SW1391a will appear and give us more insights into the minds of the prehistoric potters who created these images.

If you would like to participate in the excavation or laboratory projects at the White Mountain Archaeological Center, call or write to make reservations for your program. Your interest and excitement provides the means and the method for our continuing research.

If you have a prehistoric Southwest ceramic vessel, and this vessel exhibits what you believe to be coherent icons, I would encourage you to send photographs of the pottery for possible translation. Our symbol dictionary is to date very small. The more vessels that can be translated, the larger our icon vocabulary will become, and there will be more that we will ultimately understand about the lives of the prehistoric peoples of the Southwest.

White Mountain Archaeological Center
H C 30
St. Johns, Arizona 85936
602-333-5857

Author James R. Cunkle and staff

Preface

I began this study attempting to assemble a comprehensive volume that would allow the novice to identify the major prehistoric pottery types of the Southwest. There is no single volume currently in print. The student of Southwest ceramics must independently assemble a small library of books, each focusing upon one small area in the Southwest. I was attempting to compile all of the information necessary, i.e. temper, firing, form, provenience, color, etc. to assist the novice in the identification of several of the many prehistoric pottery types that are currently recognized as distinctive.

I spent months in the back rooms of museums and universities photographing prehistoric vessels by "type." The volume that I had in mind would have been similar to the "Field Guide to Insects", or "Minerals" or "Sea Shells". It would not have been totally comprehensive, but it would have provided the basics, the beginnings, and it would have inspired the interest necessary for the beginner to start down that long road of discovery, which is often the spark that young scientists require.

During my dusty back room investigations, I found nothing that led to the analysis found in this book. The prehistoric vessels that I photographed exhibited little or none of the iconography assembled in this volume. The pottery types were nicely grouped on the padded shelves and classified by all of the standard methods.

Fortunately, I did not limit my investigations to the storerooms of academia. I was trained as a field archaeologist, and whenever possible, I traveled to the ongoing field investigations being conducted in the Southwest to examine the most recent ceramic material being excavated.

While in the field in the summer of 1990, a vessel was unearthed that changed the entire direction of my research. It opened my eyes to a world of information previously muddied beneath the usual analytical methods used to investigate prehistoric Southwest pottery.

It was a Fourmile bowl (A.D. 1325-1400) (cover photo) discovered in the White Mountains of Arizona, catalogued as SW1391a, that ignited a wildfire. A subtle Rosetta Stone that tells a story.

There are clearly as many as ten glyphs, combined on the interior of the bowl, that relate to the viewer a legend that was widely known prehistorically. By comparing these ten glyphs with other ceramics from the same site and other sites in the White Mountains area, several other unit icons were discovered.

These icons are combined in ways that clearly indicate the embryonic stages of a written language.

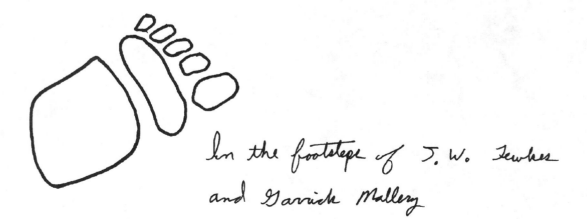

In the footsteps of J. W. Fewkes
and Garrick Mallery

Contents

Room 26, North Pueblo, Raven Site Ruin

Restoration, curation

Introduction

The designs found on the prehistoric pottery of the Southwest have previously been analyzed with little attention given to the elemental units which make up the patterns. This is understandable, because the majority of these designs are not relevant to this research. They do not exhibit icons in meaningful relationships. The basements and back rooms of museums and universities are crammed with ceramics that are beautifully executed, but have few elements of design that are anything other than aesthetically pleasing.

In 1987, excavations were begun at Raven Site Ruin located on the northern edges of the White Mountains in Arizona (see map, page 4, figure 1.) The site was prehistorically one of the major populational centers along the Little Colorado River and was occupied from as early as A.D. 1000 with continuous habitation until as late as A.D. 1450. The excavations to date indicate the two distinct ceramic traditions may have evolved at Raven Site Ruin. The first of these traditions were the White Mountain Redwares. This pottery sequence begins with the Puerco Black-on-red vessels at around A.D. 1000 and continues through a progression of pottery types most of which are found at Raven Site. This sequence terminates at the site with the Fourmile Polychrome pottery vessels at A.D. 1380. The second ceramic tradition which may have evolved at the site, are the vitreous Zuni glazewares.

The vessels excavated at Raven Site Ruin which are part of the White Mountain Redware ceramic tradition, exhibit symbols with not only a clear unit meaning, but these symbols are often combined to communicate far more than aesthetics. The Fourmile Polychrome vessels which are the climax of the White Mountain Redware tradition found at Raven Site, display the majority of this iconography. The vitreous Zuni glazewares which are also found on the site, exhibit less iconography.

Interestingly, nearly all of the Fourmile Polychrome material so far excavated at Raven Site has been extremely fragmentary. A small part of a vessel will be discovered at a very shallow provenience. A year or two later, with the excavation of nearby rooms in the same area, more sherds of that same vessel will appear during cleaning and analysis. Over several years of excavation at the north end of the site, Fourmile Polychrome vessels reluctantly emerge piece by piece. These vessels seem to have been deliberately splattered over large areas of the site. This could be the result of prehistoric or historic vandals smashing surface ceramics. However, Cushing observed a ceremony during his stay with the Zuni that may account for this phenomenon. During certain Katsina ceremonies, the Katsina clowns would go from house to house in the pueblo and smash pottery of the finest type in a ritual killing. These vessels were purposely left outside the roof entrances of the houses to accommodate the clowns (Cushing 1901.) If a ceremony of this kind occurred prehistorically at Raven Site Ruin, it could account for the poor condition and wide provenience of the Fourmile material.

Excavation at the site indicates a large populational exodus between A.D. 1350-1380 . The potters who produced the Fourmile Polychromes moved north, very possibly to the Homolovi Ruin near Winslow, Arizona. Fourmile Polychromes of the same fine quality are found at Homolovi, but they are made from local clays and tempers. These population movements are well documented (Fewkes 1895:267, Hodge 1907-10, et al) The White Mountain Redwares are believed to be ancestral to several other pottery types, including the Sikyatki ceramics to the north and the Salado Polychromes to the south (Fewkes 1895, Steen 1966.) Raven Site Ruin was not abandoned. Vitreous Zuni glazewares continued to be produced, but the White Mountain Redwares tradition ended.

The majority of pottery discussed in this volume, which exhibits iconography, was excavated at Raven Site Ruin. Other examples are included that were found to the south, below the Mogollon Rim, along the prehistoric trade routes which connected Raven Site with other contemporaneous populational centers.

Do these icons represent a written language?

This analysis of the iconographic representations on pottery vessels will identify a list of symbols. They will be understood to represent what they are, i.e. clouds, wind, mountains, etc. Many of the symbols presented here are not new to academia.

The swastika representing the four directions or the checkerboard pattern representing the Milky Way are examples of icons with meanings that few would debate. This study will attempt to expand the known list of symbols and to demonstrate how these were used to convey a much larger meaning than was previously hypothesized. The first step in the process is to recognize the symbols in their basic unit form. The second step is to identify them when they are clustered with associated icons. When several identified icons are used together, they often produce an image as straightforward as "cloud"-"wind"-"rain" over "mountain"-"earth". Combinations such as these will often comprise the entire theme of the vessel. There will be nothing else present to postulate a further meaning, other than perhaps a nice landscape. This is the norm on prehistoric pottery found in the Southwest that exhibit any icons at all. Attractive combinations appear with good execution and beautiful symmetry, but lacking any clues which would indicate a deeper symbolism.

By identifying the individual icons, the building blocks of translation begin to appear. When the rare occasion presents itself and a vessel is discovered with icon combinations that have not previously been observed, it is then possible to attempt to translate what these unknown combinations could represent. Because the majority of vessels that exhibit icons display easily recognizable, coherent combinations, it would be erroneous to dismiss unrecognizable combinations as gibberish. An icon by its very nature is a recognized meaningful unit. We still use them today. The buttons on your remote control have arrows that indicate direction. The doors of rest rooms indicate gender segregation with anthropomorphic symbols. There has recently been a flood of new information suggesting that the symbols found on the rock art of the Southwest may be much more than the "mindless doodles of ignorant savages". Many of the symbols found on these petroglyphs are now believed to indicate the location of springs, caves, trails and other petroglyphic panels (Martineau 1987.)

This study will examine petroglyphic representations and will compare these with the symbols found on the ceramics.

The pottery icons of the White Mountains are pictographic representations. The symbols used to represent clouds will usually look like clouds, allowing for the limits of the media in which they were produced and the inherent style of the designs. A pictographic representation, although rudimentary as a language form, does have a phonetic value. The prehistoric people who created the symbol spoke. They had a verbal ability as complex as any human group. They spoke a word for "cloud", or more likely several words. This automatically involves phonetics into the symbol system, even though the leap to pure phonetic representation probably was not achieved. If phonetic representations were the dominant symbols, one would expect to find linear sequences of symbols. Phonetic representations may be present in the iconography of the prehistoric Southwest, although the translation of these probable phonetic representations is beyond the scope of this study.

Key signs or determinatives, signs with a conceptual value but that are not pronounced, are an integral part of all symbol systems (Knorosov 1952). These appear in the iconography of the prehistoric Southwest, most obviously by the positioning of the individual icons. Another probable determinative is the redundancy found in this symbol system. The arrow point head of the thunderbird on the cover of this volume is repeated within the head of the bird. This repetition appears to be used for emphasis. One is reminded of the Pima word "Hohokam". "Hokam" means "used up" and "Hohokam" translates "all used up". The arrow point head of the thunderbird translates "powerful" or "able to cause harm". The repeated/redundant arrow point translates "very powerful". There are probably other key signs or determinatives that resist modern translation.

The White Mountain Redwares will occasionally exhibit two or more icons in combination that produce a meaning beyond the individual icons value. Many examples will be demonstrated both in the section "Vessel Translations" and "The Icons." Do these symbol combinations represent a written language? The evidence speaks as clearly as the icons.

Form, color and number.

When speaking of symbolism and its application, there is symbolism of form, color and number. In the case of prehistoric Southwest pottery, color is limited to the technology of the ceramics involved. Certainly in the case of the White Mountain Redwares, the ceramic vehicle was less restricting than in earlier times. Beginning in A.D. 1180 with the introduction of the Wingate Polychromes and continuing even into the post-Fourmile Polychrome period after A.D. 1400, not only were multi-colored slips applied and polished, but glazes including the brilliant colors of the copper and magnesium based vitreous varieties were used with excellent execution. The development of these polychrome pottery types may have been instrumental in the observed blossoming of the iconography portrayed on these ceramics. But ceramics as a vehicle to carry the icons does limit the kind of color classifications that may have truly been used in the larger prehistoric culture. There are many examples of the use of color as primary to the understanding of symbolic representations in the Southwest. The Navajo have specific colors that are used in sandpainting depictions which are associated with a myriad of related elements, most specifically the four directions, male and female, religious localities and specific deities. The Zuni as recorded in the nineteenth century used specific colors in association with the four directions and nadir, zenith and center. It is a common characteristic of human kind to relate specific colors with larger ideograms. Blue is for boys, pink is for girls, white is good, black is bad and violet is passionate. To a modern Westerner, this is common knowledge; it would pass virtually unnoticed because of its overuse. It is fairly safe to speculate that prehistoric peoples of the Southwest used specific colors in association with specific ideas and icons. The extent of these color associations may never be accurately known because so much of the color of prehistoric material is lost to poor preservation or was originally absent because of the limits of the media.

Much of this text is dedicated to the form of the icons. By comparing the form, i.e. shapes, combinations, etc. of known icons throughout the history and protohistory of the Southwest, the leap into the translation of the prehistoric forms is made. When the form of the icon bears resemblance to the actual thing being represented, translation is aided. However, icons change. A symbol that may have been graphic in A.D. 1200 could transpose into a stylized outline by A.D. 1380, or the opposite could occur. Distance from the source of origin can alter a symbol's appearance. The need to cram more information onto the small area of the interior of a bowl or the rim of a jar could cause symbols to be reduced in form which could deter their interpretation. The form of the icon can be confusing or enlightening.

Only on rare occasions in the prehistoric pottery record are vessels found that display the right mix of graphic depiction and stylized glyph whereby the meaning of the icons are not polemic. The "Smoking Gun", vessel SW1391a (cover photo), is just such an instance. The thunderbird looks like a bird, but is composed of unit elements that have unit meaning. The bird's wings are clouds, there is a glyph that translates "flight" attached to the wing, the pueblo below the bird is made up of components that are sufficiently graphic to be identified.

While examining iconography of the Southwest, number values cannot be ignored. Whole studies have centered on the question, "how many?". With the recent surge of archaeoastronomy this question has been labored. Petroglyphs and ceramics have been re-examined seeking lunar and solar numbers. Dr. Robbins of the University of Texas, Austin, examines the possibility that many of the prehistoric vessels produced by the Mimbres potters around A.D. 1000 may depict solar and lunar events quite possibly including the explosion of the crab nebula in A.D. 1054 (see appendix I). Dr. Robbins has deduced many lunar numbers associated with the key glyph on these prehistoric bowls. Depictions of the rabbit are the instrumental flags that alert researchers to the possibility of lunar representations (see appendix I). Solar representations and their associated numerology are also being sought. However, the key glyph has not positively been identified. Representations of deer could be the key symbol for the sun, as rabbits are for the moon (Schele 1977, Thompson 1967), however, so far no "Smoking Gun" vessel has been found. Deer are associated with the sun in Mayan art and the trade and cultural connections between the Mimbrenos and the Meso-Americans are seldom debated. The use of specific symbolic numbers can be demonstrated throughout the known cultures of the Southwest. The most predominant single number in the whole of the Southwest cultures, Pueblo, Athapaskan, and most likely prehistoric, is the number four. Never in any other collections of mythology have I seen a number so repeated. There are other numbers that held significance, but the number four is so overused by the Hopi, the Zuni and the Navajo, to name a few, that it cannot be ignored as represented on the prehistoric record (Mullet 1979, Cushing 1901, Reichard 1977, et al). In Pueblo mythology, this is the fourth world into which man emerged through the sipapu.

The overuse of the number four in the Southwest probably evolved from this belief. The icon representing the four directions, the swastika, has long been recognized as a meaningful glyph which embodies the number four. This glyph is examined specifically in the icon section of this text.

The Zuni divided the world into seven. The principle division is again the four directions plus zenith, nadir and center. The seven divisions each have associated colors: north is yellow, west is blue, south is red, east is white, the upper region is many colored, the lower region is black and the center has all colors.

The Navajo in their sandpainting rituals use a system that suspiciously resembles the Zuni classifications. Again the principle number is four, based on the four directions, and again the upper regions and lower regions are recognized. Five is also an important numerical representation in Navajo sandpaintings, and their use of color also mirrors the Zuni.

This text attempts the translation of icons found on pottery that is centuries old. Culture(s) that produced the pottery used no known written records other than the icon combinations themselves. The clues to the icon meaning are scant. Recent excavations in the White Mountains area have unearthed vessels with positive indicators which assist the translation of the glyphs. Many of these vessels are presented here.

An advantage of pottery over petroglyphs in the translation of symbols.

One of the inherent problems in the translation of petroglyphs is the current inability to date the panels. It is impossible to know for sure who carved what when (Schaafsma 1980). When viewing a petroglyph, it is not possible to conclude which markings are contemporaneous and which were carved earlier or later, with the possible exception of the vandalous markings produced by the early settlers and modern tourists. Various techniques have been attempted to date the panels including desert varnish measurement and pigment analysis in the case of pictographs, but so far none have been totally satisfactory (Barnes 1982). Pottery transcends this dilemma. A prehistoric pottery vessel was produced at one point in time and probably by one craftswoman. Any symbols found on the same vessel are obviously contemporaneous, and their

meaning would be understood during the temporal period of that pottery's production. Pottery typing in the Southwest has been used as a dating technique so extensively that with the correlation of dendrochronology from other sites, it is often used as the primary tool to date sites unless good beam material is available. An icon on a pottery vessel can be correlated with a calendar date often within as short a temporal span as 50 to 100 years. It's interesting to note that the iconography at Raven Site is most prevalent during a very brief period. The Tularosa Black-on-white material appears around A.D. 1200, and demonstrates occasional icon use. The peak period is during the Fourmile Polychrome pottery production, which seems to have terminated at Raven Site by the year A. D. 1380. The appearance and use of meaningful icons on pottery at Raven Site seems to have lasted, at best, less than two centuries.

The basic building blocks.

Chart II illustrates many of the prehistoric glyphs that have been isolated during this study and the research of hundreds of others. The pages following will elaborate on each individual glyph and will cite the sources used in the interpretations. Many photographic examples are given.

The geometric forms used to represent various icons seem to be quite consistent. In the translations thus far, no contradictions of basic forms have been encountered. Some forms are quite specific such as squares and rectangles representing "property/human created space", and the equilateral triangle for "arrow point". Others, such as the spiral, seem to be used to represent various ideas.

Equilateral triangle. This form almost exclusively indicates an "arrow point" icon. In combined form, its meaning is extended to indicate "war", "siege", "hurt/harm/kill", "not hurt/harmed/killed".

Right triangle. This form is almost exclusively used to illustrate "mountains" and "clouds". It is not difficult to visualize the similarities between the two. The icon for "mountain" will also often contain the "earth/land" icon, and the "cloud" triangle will often be associated with other weather elements such as "wind", "rain" and "flight".

Square or rectangle. This form almost unequivocally indicates "property/ownership", "geographical place", "human created/controlled space". Nature does not make squares and rectangles, humankind does. This glyph with this meaning is found virtually worldwide. It is very often seen combined with clan symbols in petroglyph use to indicate property markers, i.e. "no trespassing" signs.

Unilateral terrace. This form is used in a variety of ways which often causes confusion as to its indicated meaning. Two of these units are seen interlocked in the "house/marriage" icon. It is used in multiple interlocked units to indicate the multiple households, or possibly just the multiple buildings in the "pueblo" icon. It is used in isolation often to indicate a cloud form, including a high degree of frequency as the "cloud/wings" of thunderbirds. It is often seen interlocked, one unit with the "earth/land" icon, and one unit solid or negative, without any additional information (see photo 1). In this case the symbol very much resembles the Tao symbol "Yin and Yang" indicating balance and harmony in nature through combined male and female elements. A more reasonable translation for this combination found on the pottery of the Southwest could be an "earth/sky" glyph. F. H. Cushing observed in the nineteenth century that the Zuni used a terraced symbol to represent the earth, and an inverted terrace to represent the sky. One of the unilateral terraced units in this combination always contains the "earth/land" glyph; this unit could, therefore, represent the "earth" and the other solid/negative unit could represent the "sky". This same treatment is observed in the distinguishing features inherent to "mountain" and "cloud" icons.

Parallel lines. This form almost exclusively indicates "earth/land". There are variations of this form. Some parallel lines are diagonal within another icon. Some sets of parallel lines are much wider, having up to a dozen lines, and some are narrow with as few as two. The wider vertical sets in certain context may indicate "safety", according to modern Hopi glyph translations. No unique meaning is known for diagonal sets.

Spirals. The spiral indicates a traveling motion. Movement is downward or upward depending upon the direction of the spiral. This is consistent with the use of the spiral at the Fajada Butte Sun Dagger site. The sun and moon appear to ascend and descend. Spirals forming a square or rectangle found on petroglyphs may indicate, according to some authors, "descending/ascending onto property". Spirals are very often used to indicate wind and the "motion" of wind when combined with other weather elements. This form

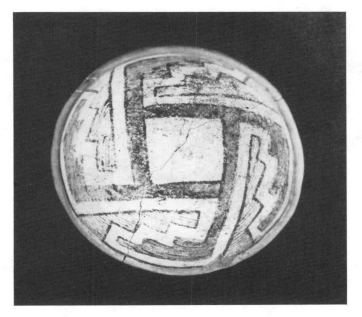

Photo 1. Pinto Polychrome bowl excavated to the south of Raven Site Ruin showing interlocked unilateral terraced units, one with the parallel lines which represent "earth" and the other unit solid which indicates "sky". Notice that the solid unit which would represent the sky is also the classic unilateral cloud form. All four of the "cloud/sky" icons on this bowl in combination also create the "swastika" or "four directions" glyph.

is also used as an icon for "smoke". Again, the motion of the swirling smoke is the key to the icon.

Circles. Circles are used to indicate "enclosure", 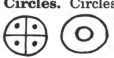 "something there". They are often used to indicate an area, a field of play. The circle icon combined with a cross, and sometimes a cross and dots, indicates "something divided", very similar to our modern mathematical symbol.

Dots. Dots almost always indicate "water", "rain", "wet". Protohistorically, many tribes illustrated the devastation of smallpox with dots (Mallery 1888-89).

From these basic forms the prehistoric Southwest Indians combined icons into secondary and tertiary meanings, developing illustrative narratives on many of the White Mountain Redwares pottery types.

Method of translation.

In order to attempt the translation of the icons encountered, all diagnostic tools will be used. Ethnographic material, petroglyphs, pictographs, sign language both historic and protohistoric, Katsina lore and any other vehicle that renders itself as relevant to the translation will be employed.

What seemed at first to be the most relevant ethnographic records to examine are the Zuni legends and customs as recorded by Frank Hamilton Cushing in the nineteenth century (Cushing 1901). Zuni pueblo is located less than one hundred miles north of the Raven Site where the majority of the vessels exhibiting iconography are being excavated. Zuni pueblo to the north was occupied prehistorically during the same temporal period as the later phases of Raven Site Ruin. Because many of the ceramic depictions illustrate a narrative, it could be possible that Cushing recorded legends that mirror those represented on ceramics centuries earlier. Following the examination of the Zuni legends, the next logical ethnographic candidates were the legends of the Hopi Indians. These too were examined. After comparing the legends of the Zuni, Hopi and even the Athapaskan speakers, the Navajo, through their sandpainting rituals, a remarkable similarity between all of the legends was observed. There were variations in the legends between these groups, but common themes, protagonists and places were repeated again and again.

After examining the legends of the major Southwest cultural groups, it became clear that these cultures were greatly entwined. This melding can be carried into the prehistoric record by examining one of the most common, recurring themes. In Zuni legend there are two mischievous twins who rid the world of monsters and manage to get themselves into a great deal of trouble in the process.

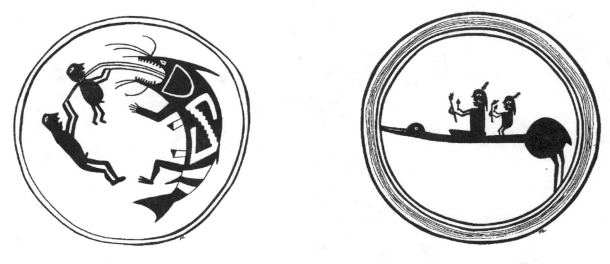

Figure 2   Figure 3

Figures 2 and 3. Mimbres Classic Black-on-white bowls showing the warrior twins (2) recovering the rains from the Cloud Swallower and (3) riding on the neck of a crane. (From LeBlanc 1983, Moulard 1984)

These beings are named Ahaiyuta and Matsailema. In Hopi legend the same two deities are up to the same waggish behavior and they are named Puukonhoya and Palunhoya. Found in the mythology surrounding the Navajo sandpainting ceremonies these beings appear again, exhibiting the same behavior and named "slayer of alien gods" and "child of the water" respectively. The stories of these warrior twins share many common elements regardless of which cultural group is relating the story. To carry the twins back into prehistory is easily accomplished. Many hundreds of Mimbres Classic pottery bowls dating from A.D. 1000 unmistakably illustrate these twins up to their usual tricks, slaying monsters, riding cranes and seducing young maidens (see figures 2 and 3). The evidence of the twins in modern legend and also in the prehistoric record demonstrates only one of the possible continuities that probably exist.

After examining Indian legends for clues to the translation of pottery icons, attention was directed to sign language, both proto-historic and modern. I believe the gestural representations produced when signing relate very directly with both the symbols on pictographs and petroglyphs, and with the icons found on prehistoric pottery. This idea is not entirely new. Garrick Mallery in his report to the Smithsonian Institution in the nineteenth century observed many similarities between the two forms, gestural and two dimensional. More recently, LaVan Martineau made the comparison in his analysis (Mallery 1879, Martineau 1987). Sign language gestures represent things and ideas in their most easily recognized and performable unit form. They have to be, otherwise it would increase the difficulty of basic communication between those using the system. Icons also represent a thing or idea reduced to its simplest recognizable and performed, i.e. drawn, painted or carved, unit form. This may partly be due to the difficult media used to create the depictions. Rock is not the easiest thing on which to carve a narrative illustration, nor does the surface of a ceramic vessel give you the latitude of papyrus or other more advanced representational media. Egyptian hieroglyphics became a flowing, realistic form because of the forgiving medium of papyrus, whereas cuneiform became rigid, non-realistic and stylized because of the limiting medium of wet clay and the stylus (Senner 1989). Both sign language and iconography employ the *lingua franca* of basic human behavior which has remained largely unchanged for centuries. We still hear through two ears, see through two eyes, walk upright, and everybody urinates. This analysis relies upon these unchanged basic human behaviors. If the behaviors of human groups are largely unchanged, then the gestures and iconographic symbols used to represent those behaviors visually should be similar and comparable, both in their representations gestural and two dimensional.

When symbols are combined, they convey not only their individual meanings, but also a further meaning because of the combination.

In most cases in iconography, many different symbols with the same meaning are used together to reenforce the thought or theme in the depiction. This is also very true in petroglyphs and pictographs. A panel with a "war" theme may contain various "war" icons several times to reenforce the theme and guarantee its clarity (see figure 4). This

Figure 4. Petroglyph panel with the icon for "war" repeated to clarify the meaning. (From Martineau 1973)

Photo 2. SW1013 Fourmile Polychrome bowl 1325-1400 A.D. showing three different "water/rain" icons to reenforce meaning. This practice greatly aids in icon translation, revealing several icons with identical meanings on a single "Thesaurus" vessel. It is not surprising that the prehistoric Southwest Indians had so many water/rain symbols. It was very important to them. Without the rains, people starved.

practice of repeating icons to reenforce and clarify the meaning gives the translator a powerful tool. Because of this practice, pottery will often present several variations of the same icon, with the same general meaning on one vessel. This enables the translator to see several examples of the same icon in one place, produced and understood by the same author, during one temporal period. The various icons for "water/rain" are a good example. Vessel SW1013 exhibits three separate icons for "water/rain": 1, the ticking around the circles in the center of the bowl, 2, the dots in the "clouds" around the inside rim of the bowl, 3, the dots within the "earth/land" icon on the exterior of the vessel (see SW1013 photo 2 and "water/rain" icon translation). This redundancy in symbol use on a single narrative is also a key utilized in the translation of Mayan glyphs. Discovering glyphs with like meaning is made possible often because the author repeats the meaning using a semantic equivalent (Lounsbury 1989). By knowing the meaning of one or more of the icons from other sources, it is then possible to

Figure 5

Figure 6

Figures 5 and 6. Mimbres Black-on-white bowls which illustrate a story/legend/fable.
(From Moulard 1984, Brody 1977)

deduce similar meanings from the icons with similar attributes. As the list of icons with known meaning grows, the ability to translate other icons also expands. When a symbol has been interpreted, and when there is a great amount of certainty that it has been correctly translated, then an attempt is made to translate icons that are associated with the "known" symbol. At this point, special attention is also given to units within the "known" icon. Many symbols are made up of smaller ones. Translate the larger symbol, and the smaller symbols within are illuminated. This method also works in reverse, i.e. look for what the combined/associated meaning might be when groups of unit icons are observed. This process of interpretation by analyzing the unit parts of a "known" icon is logical, but far from perfect. If an error is made in the initial step, several symbols may be incorrectly translated. Caution is exercised not to stray too far from the original symbol and its translation.

Vessel SW1391a and its near twin from Sikyatki (see "The Smoking Gun") also demonstrate the nature of many of the depictions found on prehistoric pottery of the Southwest. These symbols, in combination, seem to be an illustration to a known narrative. There is a story behind the illustration; a story that is common knowledge, i.e. a fable or legend. This is often the case of Classic Mimbres Black-on-white pottery, although the use of icons is not their primary vehicle of communication on the vessels. The figures are involved in actions that depict a tale, repeatedly told (see figures 5, 6 and cover). Mixtex and the Central Mexican Codices are of a similar nature. Their method of narration is fundamentally a serial pictorial. The pottery vessels of the White Mountains are pictorials composed of unit symbols, with not only singular symbol meaning, but also meanings created by combining the icons to produce meanings not present when the icons are in isolation.

Sign language, one helpful tool.

One tool which aids in these translation attempts is a language system that incorporates many of the elemental units found in prehistoric iconography. Sign language is a system of unit ideas, gestural images, quickly and easily formed, but beautifully blended to encompass the whole spectrum of human emotion and intelligence. Sign language was utilized across North America. Because of the continent's vast area and small, iso-

lated populations, many dialectic and linguistic boundaries evolved (Mallery 1879-80:311). It is estimated that in the sixteenth century, there were over two thousand languages used on the continent. It is documented when contact was made prehistorically between groups on the North American continent, sign language was employed to communicate between groups which lacked any other common language. This phenomenon was observed by the early fur traders and military parties who first penetrated these areas and made initial contact with these Indian groups. Their Indian guides would often communicate with other Indian groups using a sign language that appeared to have quite a universal comprehension. The idea that sign language was widely used across the Americas should not be surprising. If the use of sign language was observed by the first Europeans who made contact with the Indians on the North American continent, then it is fairly safe to speculate that it was being used prehistorically. It may have been a *lingua franca* understood and utilized by a large percentage of the North American Indian tribes. Due to their contact with many linguistic clusters, it would be especially essential to those groups with a high degree of mobility, such as the prehistoric Pochteca traders and more recently the Plains Indians aided by the introduction of the horse. By comparing modern American gestures used by the deaf, and protohistoric sign language used across North America as recorded by the Spanish conquistadors arriving from the South and West, and early settlers and military personnel from the East, to the two dimensional symbols found on pictographs, petroglyphs, and pottery, a similarity is observed. This is not a one to one correlation. This is not observed on all pottery. It does not always work. However, with a great many icons the correlation is convincing and statistically valid.

The reason why a comparison between modern sign language and prehistoric sign language and then two dimensional representation may be possible is because a great many basic human operations such as eating, drinking, hearing, seeing, etc., remain unchanged. The purpose of sign language today and in the past is to quickly and as simply as possible convey ideas between people who have no other way to communicate. The gestures used when signing easily transpose into two dimensional symbols which are also readily understood. If the basic sign language gestures have remained largely unchanged through time, then they should help reveal the meaning of icons created centuries ago.

During the nineteenth century, North American Indians were "shown" like zoo animals as a novelty across Europe.

"They showed the greatest pleasure in meeting deaf-mutes, precisely as travelers in a foreign country are rejoiced to meet persons speaking their language, with whom they can hold direct communication (by means of signing) without the tiresome and often suspected medium of an interpreter." (Mallery 1879-80: 321).

Certainly the sign language used by the North American Indians of the nineteenth century is not identical to modern signing or prehistoric signing, but sufficient similarities may exist because of basic, unchanging human activities and behaviors that would allow, not only the comparison, but would quite possibly permit actual communication between the groups utilizing the gestures. The leap from sign language gestures to the icons found on prehistoric pottery would seem untenable. Certainly attempting a direct comparison based solely on sign language would be vastly inconclusive. The purpose here is to translate the icons on the pottery. The best place to begin is with the icons themselves and their relationship to one another as they are observed on the pottery vessels. Sign language is only one tool to employ.

Purpose

The purpose of this study is to alert ceramicists to the possibility that the symbols and symbol combinations encountered on prehistoric Southwest pottery may, in some cases, contain meaning beyond mere aesthetics. If this study causes ceramicists to begin to look at the pottery with that possibility in mind, then this study will have achieved its purpose.

In this study the following terms will be used accordingly:

- **Symbol,** something that represents something else by association, resemblance or convention.
- **Icon,** an image or representation, an ideogram, or ideograph, a character or symbol representing an idea or thing without expressing a particular word or phrase for it, as the characters in Chinese.
- **Logogram,** or logograph, a symbol or letter representing an entire word.

- **Emblem,** an object or depiction of an object that comes to represent something else, usually by suggesting its nature or history. A distinctive badge, design or device.

These definitions are straight out of Webster's Third New International Dictionary. It is not my intent to spend needless pages lamenting the weaknesses of modern semantics. These terms are virtually interchangeable for the purposes of our discussion, the only exception being "emblem" which is primarily used during the discussion of clan symbols and is not really a synonym with the other terms. One term you will not find used in this discussion is "morpheme". Morpheme is a linguistic term. It cannot be interchanged with icon, ideogram, etc., simply because it refers to language even though the basic meaning of the term is similar to the others. There is no evidence to suggest that the symbols on prehistoric Southwest pottery are phonetic. They had a phonetic value prehistorically, just as any symbol used in any culture shares a spoken, i.e. pronounced representation alongside the silently understood meaning of the symbol. The problem with attempting to discover any phonetic value to the icons lies with the fact that we have very limited information of the languages spoken in the prehistoric Southwest. There have been attempts in the past to interpret prehistoric designs using linguistics, however, better interpretive tools may exist.

The total number of prehistoric glyphs that share interpretive acceptance in the academic community can be counted on one hand. This study reiterates those symbols, and brings to light many more. The total symbol dictionary assembled in this study is still less than thirty glyphs. One might argue that this small number of symbols could never constitute the makings of a written language. However, we must keep in mind the limits of the archaeological record. Preservation is the demon that murks the waters. When a prehistoric Southwest site is excavated, there is only a tiny percentage of cultural material that survives the ravages of time. Even in the best preservation conditions, which rarely exist, the archaeologist can conserve less than ten percent of the total cultural record. We excavate lithic material, ceramic, bone, shell, an occasional mural and very little fabric, basketry or wood. The actual number is more probably one percent or less of the entire cultural index. Few would argue with the ten percent figure. This means that instead of thirty symbols, the culture actually used and recognized three hundred glyphs. If you are bold enough to accept the one percent variable, then the total number of coherent, exercised symbols ranges in the thousands. A culture with thousands of unit symbols, their combinations, key signs and phonetic nuances is exercising a written language by any modern skeptic's standards.

Some of the interpretations of the symbols presented here may be wrong. Every possible clue to the icon's meanings is utilized, every source of information has been sought, historic, protohistoric and prehistoric, to help unravel unknown meanings.

In this study, the use of quotation marks, "....." simply indicates that the icon translations are not one hundred percent certain. Barring the possibility of the invention of a time machine and direct contact verification with the people who produced the symbols, the quotation marks will remain.

Vessel translations are presented first. Vessel translations consist of all of the icons found on a single vessel in association, and their possible combined meanings. Being a cynical observer, I understand that many of you reading this text will initially scoff at many of the vessel translations. Keep reading. Toward the end of this book, each individual icon is analyzed individually. These appear in alphabetical order, "arrow point" through "wind". This causes some redundancy, but is necessary for overall clarity. In order to isolate the icon in question in the photographic examples, an illustration appears at the right of the photograph. In the illustration, the icon being reviewed is drawn with broader, darker lines, and any associated icon(s) are drawn with thinner, lighter lines.

While reading the text, you will frequently come across references to figures and photos. Figures are sequential numbering 1 through 121 and photos are independently sequential numbering 1 through 105. Be sure to notice whether the reference calls for a figure or a photo.

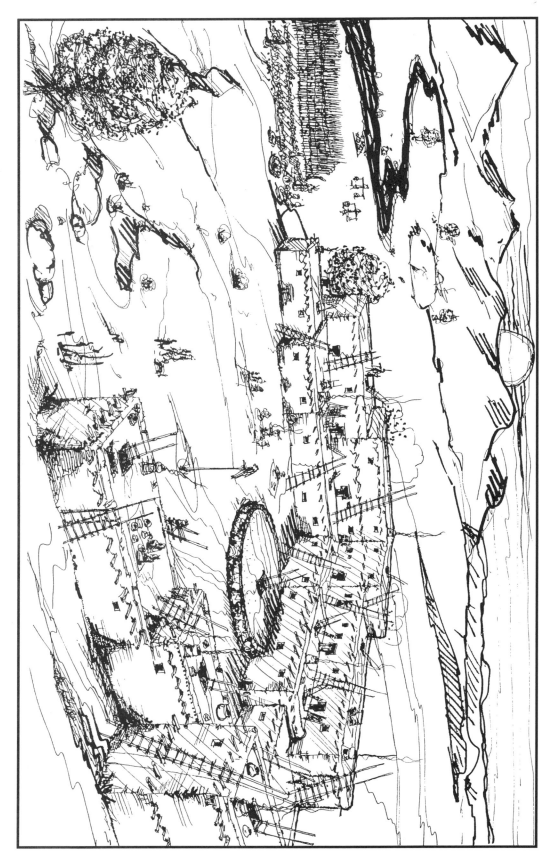

Artist's rendition of the South Pueblo at Raven Site Ruin, 1425 A.D.

Chapter I

The Smoking Gun

Vessel SW1391a
(Cover Photo)

In the summer of 1990 during the analysis of ceramic material from the Raven Site Ruin, a Fourmile Polychrome bowl grew out of the surface of the lab table. It illustrated a narrative. This vessel, SW1391a, caused quite a debate, and subsequently this ongoing research project. The bowl is unquestionably authentic. It was excavated from the floor of room #20. Room #20 was occupied around A.D. 1380-1400 and possibly even after A.D. 1400, dates somewhat later than the presence of Fourmile ceramics would indicate. However, it is believed that vessel SW1391a was brought from the older pueblo to the north, near datums 4 and 5. This older pueblo found on the same hill had a populational peak around A.D. 1250, centering temporally with the Tularosa ceramic phase. It is believed that the Fourmile material found on the entire site, including the south city, room #20, and vessel SW1391a, were produced by the women of the north city toward the end of its populational climax and also at the height of ceramic technology occurring temporally around A.D. 1380 with the production of not only the Fourmile Polychromes but also St. Johns, Heshotauthla, Springerville, Cedar Creek, etc. The Fourmile style is only one of a multitude of ceramic types which display the pinnacle of ceramic technology in the White Mountain area.

Vessel SW1391a exhibits all of the Fourmile Polychrome ceramic characteristics (Carlson 1970) such as black banding lines edged in white kaolin, etc., and the bowl is clearly typical of the ceramic type, but what startled curators when the bowl was assembled after cleaning was the interior design. On the bowl interior is the depiction of a thunderbird flying over a pueblo below. The representation was remarkable because it was graphic enough to easily recognize the nature of the story being depicted. However, the bird and the pueblo were composed of symbolic units with specific meanings. These units could then be compared with other vessels and aid in other translations.

It was not the depiction of the thunderbird which at first caused excitement, but instead, the representation of the pueblo below the bird. It was, in fact, several months before the pueblo glyph was recognized. The vessel sat on a lab shelf gathering dust, a beautiful Fourmile, with a wonderful depiction of a thunderbird. Thunderbirds are well represented throughout prehistoric puebloan ceramic production. They are also abundantly encountered on the rock art of the Southwest. Thunderbirds are easy to recognize and several examples will follow. The icon was unquestionably important to the people who produced the glyph. The thunderbird depicted on SW1391a is of particular interest because of the combination of symbolic elements used to produce the bird, but let's begin with the analysis of the pueblo glyph which caused all of the excitement.

The representation of the pueblo below the bird is composed of four elemental units. The outline of the glyph is roughly an equilateral triangle which represents the "hill" upon which the village is built. Contained inside the triangle is a square containing interlocked terraced units. The square represents "geographical place", i.e. property, house, garden, etc., and in this case the pueblo itself which is composed of many houses. These "houses" are further represented in the glyph by the interlocked terraced units inside the square. There are four interlocked units in all, that is, "more than one". Filling the area outside the square and inside the triangle are rows of parallel lines representing "earth/land". The analysis of the "earth/land" glyph is found under the "Icon" section of this book. These parallel lines could represent crop rows. One is reminded of the "straight furrow" pattern used in quilting. It may be argued that the prehistoric pueblo people who produced this bowl may not have planted their crops in rows, however, they did irrigate, and irrigation is conducive to planting in an ordered manner. Also crops were planted outside the immediate village as represented in the glyph. More examples of the "earth/land" icon will follow, but for the moment let's look at what has been revealed by the interpretation of this one "pueblo" glyph. If this interpretation is correct, then five elemental units or icons have been discovered:

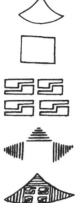

"**hill**", the triangular enclosure surrounding the total glyph.

"**human created space**", represented by the square unit inside the triangle.

"**house/marriage**", (four individual units) represented by the interlocked terraced units found inside the square.

"**earth/land**", represented by the parallel lines around the outside of the square and within the triangle.

"**pueblo/village**", all of the above.

If this analysis of the "pueblo" glyph found on vessel SW1391a is correct then several options appear, the most exciting being that basic unit icons have unit meaning which should be constant at least for the temporal period of this ceramic type's production. Other Fourmile vessels should exhibit similar icon use, possibly even the same use of the same symbols. Because these symbols are found on ceramics, instead of something more difficult to date such as the rock art of the Southwest, then we can assign a temporal span for the icons introduction, use and disuse prehistorically. Because the "pueblo" glyph is composed of several unit icons in combination, it is possible to seek out other "pueblo" glyphs on other vessels for comparison. Variations in the form of the glyph should be expected, however, the "pueblo" icon should retain a majority of the basic units.

Other vessels sharing the combination of icons that may represent "pueblo" were sought in the White Mountain Archaeological Center's collections from the Raven Site and from across the country in the repositories held by museums and other institutions. The literature was also re-examined for representations of the five icons discovered. Several other examples of the "pueblo" icon were found in the Center's collections and one remarkable representation was found in J.W. Fewkes *Designs on Prehistoric Hopi Pottery* printed in 1895 (see figure 7). The Fewkes example is particularly interesting, because the bowl illustrated displays an identical narrative as does vessel SW1391a. The two vessels may have overlapped temporally, but they were produced several hundred miles apart. The Fewkes example is a Sikyatki, basically a Jeddito, coal fired from near the present day town of Polacca on Second Mesa, undoubtedly produced by the ancestors of the Hopi. SW1391a is a Fourmile Polychrome, from a site where the producers of the Fourmile Polychromes migrated from the site, probably to the ruin of Homolovi, near present day Winslow, Arizona, around the year A.D. 1350, and then to second mesa (see vessel translation SW1509.)

The similarity between the glyphs on these two vessels may at first be difficult to recognize. Only after the entire vessel, in both cases, is examined and interpreted are the similarities clear. In the Fewkes example, "Bird With Double Eyes", the "pueblo" icon is represented below the thunderbird in a way very similar to vessel SW1391a. Once again the "hill" icon is present as a triangle surrounding the entire glyph. Within the triangle "hill" there are interlocked terraced units representing "house/marriage". These are surrounded by the square "property/geographic place" icon and the parallel lines representing "earth/land" are found above and below the interlocked terraced units. All of the elements of the combined icon "pueblo" are present and they are arranged in a manner similar to that of the Fourmile example from Raven Site. Both vessels upon translation depict a protectorate thunderbird bringing rain to the pueblo below.

With the discovery of several examples of the "pueblo" glyph found on many ceramic types separated spatially and temporally, it may therefore be possible to trace the appearance, use and disuse of the icon over space and time. Even with the finite examples encountered in the White Mountain Archaeological Center's collections sufficient representations are present to graph temporal changes in the glyph. The earliest representations are found on Tularosa Black-on-white ollas dating A. D. 1200-1300, followed by the Fourmile Polychromes dating A.D. 1325-1400, and finally the icon is seen, in context, on Gila Polychromes dating from A.D. 1200-1400 and possibly even as late as A.D. 1600 (Cordell 1984).

"hill"

"geographic place"

"house/marriage"

"earth/land"

"pueblo"

Figure 7. "Bird With Double Eyes". The hourglass body shape of the bird is interesting. This may indicate "starvation", "war", or it may even be another "water" icon as found in the water gourd form. (From Fewkes 1895)

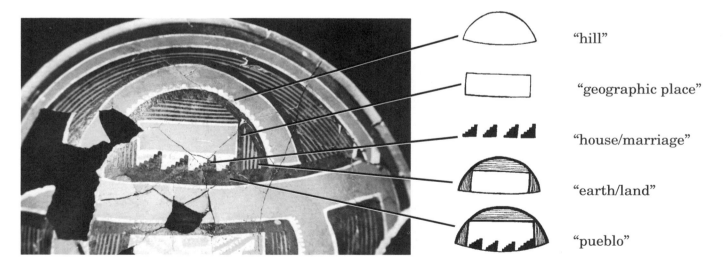

"hill"

"geographic place"

"house/marriage"

"earth/land"

"pueblo"

Photo 3. Vessel SW1012, Fourmile Polychrome bowl with the "pueblo" glyph. The terraced units in this example are repeated in profile but not interlocked, unless the white negative background constitutes the interlocked combination. (WMAC Collections)

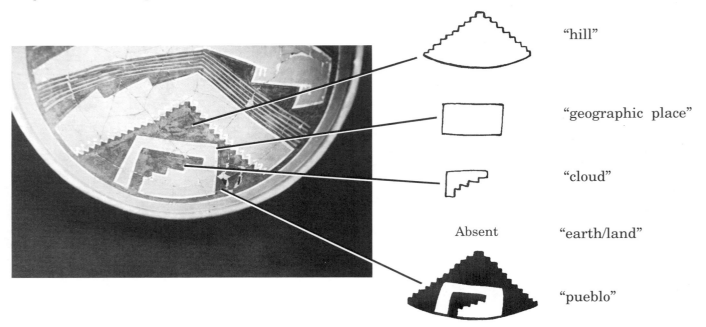

"hill"

"geographic place"

"cloud"

Absent   "earth/land"

"pueblo"

Photo 4. Vessel Pi 2. Fourmile Polychrome. This "pueblo" example contains at center a large "cloud" icon, probably representing a place name, i.e. "cloud pueblo" or the "cloud clan". (WMAC Collections)

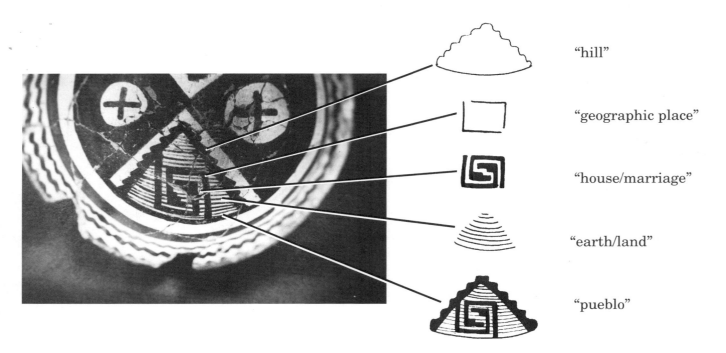

"hill"

"geographic place"

"house/marriage"

"earth/land"

"pueblo"

Photo 5. Vessel Pi 5. Gila Polychrome bowl. In this example, the "earth/land" icon runs throughout the center of the glyph. (WMAC Collections)

Chart I

Variations of the "pueblo" glyph.

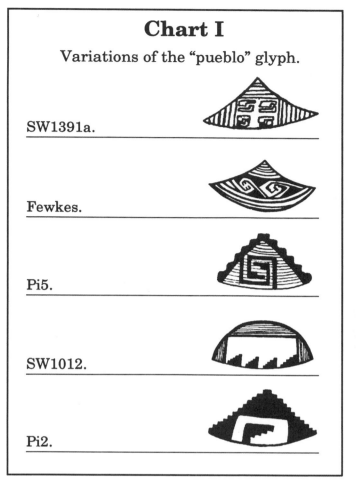

SW1391a.

Fewkes.

Pi5.

SW1012.

Pi2.

the Raven Site Ruin which is part of a Tularosa olla dating A.D. 1200-1300 (photo 6) The sherd is part of the shoulder area of the olla and it contains a pueblo glyph in a reduced form. In this example, the glyph was reduced to accommodate the small size of the representation. The triangular "hill" icon is present, also the square "geographical place" and the "earth/land". Inside the square "geographical place" icon there are three dots instead of the usual

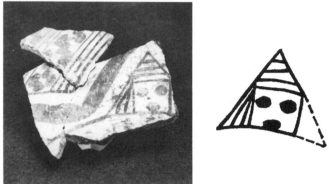

Photo 6. Tularosa sherd, R-17, Raven Site Ruin.

terraced units. With such a small "pueblo" representation, the terraced units, i.e. "house/marriage", were reduced simply to dots, that is, "more than one" of something, presumably houses as would have been illustrated by terraced units if the example had been larger.

By recognizing the basic pueblo glyph and its variations, it is then possible to focus on those variations and ascertain their individual meanings, noting which are a part of the basic pueblo depiction, and which are relating information about the individual pueblo being depicted. In the example above, the sherd from room #17 showing the three dots at center could be representing "house/ marriage" by the dots, as would be expected in a larger representation, but the information that the glyph contains says simply "three of something" or "more than one".

With the basic units of the pueblo glyph understood, it is possible to cross-check these basic units against other glyphs found on ceramics and on rock art depictions.

Granted not all of the "pueblo" glyphs exhibit all of the individual elements defined with the discovery of SW1391a. The Pi2 example lacks the "earth/land" icon and contains only a single terraced unit at center. These variations temporally and spatially should be expected. Certain elements of the basic glyph may be irrelevant to the particular pueblo being represented. With each depiction, different information concerning the pueblo is being represented which, in many cases, leaves only room in the finite space of the vessel for that information and little extra. This would mean that some of the basic units we have classified as being relevant to the "pueblo" glyph must be reduced in order to include other information, leaving just enough of the pueblo glyph intact to be recognized. This is best illustrated with a sherd excavated from

Chart II

Prehistoric Icons from the Ceramics of the White Mountains

Arrow point. Will/will not cause harm Hurt/kill/power. Hill.	
Clan symbols. Personal signatures.	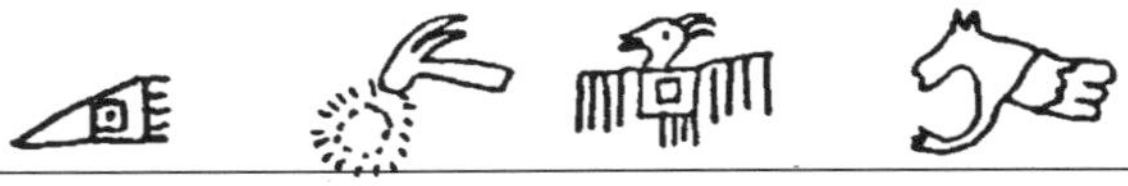
Clouds.	
Corn.	
Dead/death.	
Determined. Will not be turned away.	
Divided.	
Doorway/passageway/emergence.	
Earth/land.	
Far away.	
Flight.	
Four directions.	
House/marriage.	
Lightning. River. Serpent. Tension/confusion.	
Lizard/man.	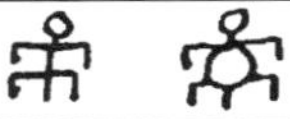
Motion. Ascend/descend.	
Mountain/hill.	
Night sky/day sky.	
Property/geographic place.	
Pueblo/village.	

Chart II (cont'd next page)

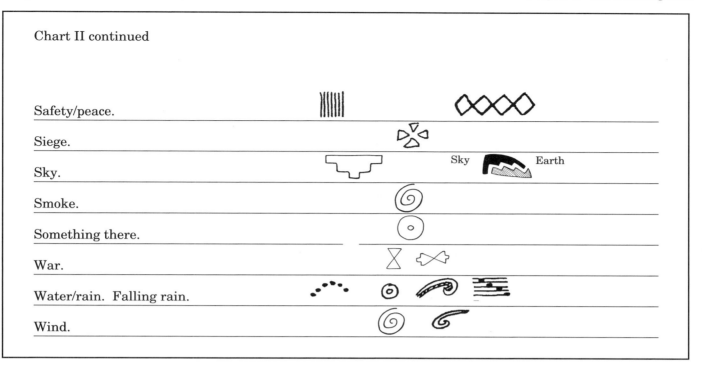

Chart II continued

Safety/peace.	
Siege.	
Sky.	Sky　Earth
Smoke.	
Something there.	
War.	
Water/rain. Falling rain.	
Wind.	

Chart II is a summary of all of the icons that have been discovered during this research. Each of these icons and their analysis are presented one by one, "arrow point" through "wind" in Chapter III. Many of these symbols and their meanings have long been recognized, others are new. Some of these new symbol interpretations may be wrong. Every attempt has been made to stay within the parameters of the data so far discovered.

With this expanded list of symbols, it is now possible to see more on the surface of Southwest ceramics than "just pretty patterns". The section which follows, "Vessel Translations", will examine several ceramic examples from the Raven Site Ruin and the surrounding White Mountains area.

For the first time in centuries, these vessels will again be able to tell their stories.

Author James R. Cunkle with ceramics unearthed
at Raven Site Ruins.

Chapter II

Vessel Translations

Photo 7. Vessel Qr15

"Storm"

This bowl is a fine example of a Salado Polychrome dating between A.D. 1200-1450. There is slight fire clouding on the red exterior and a standard black on white slipped interior. The vessel is low fired. The temper is sand/sherd and there is occasional mica content.

During the early stages of this study, the idea was entertained that both "earth" and "sky" may be represented by parallel lines, and this seemed to be confirmed by this bowl. The parallel lines are both above and below the "lightning" icon, and they at first seem to indicate that these sets of parallel lines are used for both symbols, the lightning coming from the sky and striking the earth. A common symbol for both "earth" and "sky" has also been suggested in the ancient myth and thought in Mexico (Hayden 1972). The Sahagun refers to the sun-earth as one. In Pueblo thought, the "earth" and "sky" are also often a combined idea. Arrow Grotto is referred to as an "earth/sun" shrine (Ellis and Hammack 1968). However, further comparison to other pottery vessels failed to substantiate the idea that the earth and sky are normally represented by one icon. The "sun" is not the "sky". The "sun" is often clearly represented in iconography in the prehistoric Southwest and throughout the world. The "sky" is not specifically represented with the exception of Zuni mythology, which depicts the "sky" as an inverted terrace. Things that can be found in the sky are common in prehistoric iconography. The moon, the Milky Way, stars, super nova explosions (see appendix I) clouds, even wind are very well represented, but the sky in isolation is not.

The "earth/land" symbol is well established as being represented by the parallel lines. The rows of cultigens represented in depictions of pueblos is quite certain. Also, the right triangles used for both "mountains" and "clouds" are often differentiated by parallel lines within the "mountain" icon and none in the "cloud" icon. With an abundance of "cloud" and "mountain" glyphs to reference, there has so far been no contradiction. These "earth/land" parallel lines are also found under depictions of corn plants (see photo 15). The sky in this vessel is simply represented by the space around the center set of glyphs.

The center glyph depicts two "lightning" symbols in between two "earth/land" icons. The layout of the vessel is the determining factor of why the two "earth/land" icons surround the "lightning" symbols. It is solely a matter of completing the perfect symmetry of the bowl.

The "lightning" icons are represented in positive black paint. They are wide and heavily spiked. "Lightning" icons are easily confused with other similar glyphs, such as "river" or "serpent", the zigzag motion seems to be the common element.

Surrounding the center glyph are two representations of the swirling "wind". They are solid black. The white wider swirls are "cloud" representations and are divided down their length and the lower half of the division is filled with diagonal hatchures. These diagonal hatchures represent "falling rain" and this icon is well established in White Mountains iconography. The hatchuring is on the lower side of the "cloud" icon, toward the center of the bowl. The rain falls down, toward the "earth" symbol, reenforcing the idea that the center of the bowl is "earth" and the area toward the rim of the bowl is the "sky".

"Clouds" are depicted with more mass, often resembling the icon for "mountain", and both glyphs are often difficult to distinguish except for other iconographic elements that are usually included and help clarify their meaning.

The complete and simple translation of vessel Qr15 is "storm". It is a beautiful depiction, beautiful not only because of its execution, pattern, and symmetry, but also beautiful because of the information it revealed. The icons presented are clear, related, and easily recognized. Vessel Qr15 aided in the translation of the icons for "earth/land", "wind", "falling rain", and "lightning".

The idea of "storm" has been personified in Hopi mythology. The warrior twins are aided by Hukangwaa, or the storm god, after passing a test of endurance using tobacco smoke (Mullet 1979).

In the legends of the Zuni, the eight gods of the storms transformed the warrior twins and made them more powerful than all monsters, gods or men (Cushing 1901)

Photo 8 and 8a. Vessel SW1013

"With the Rains, There is Something in Your Bowl"

This bowl is a classic Fourmile Polychrome from the Raven Site Ruin, dating A.D. 1325-1400. It is small, beautiful and it is covered with icons for "rain/water". Half of this vessel was originally excavated from room #14 in 1985. In the years that followed, rooms #15, #16 and #17 were also excavated and in each of these rooms a few more sherds of this bowl were discovered. Because of its scattered provenience, this bowl is believed to have been prehistorically broken and strewn across a large area of the site. With the completion of each dig season, we eagerly analyze the pottery material recovered in the hope of finding still more of this wonderful bowl.

SW1013 demonstrates the classic Fourmile Polychrome design, with two wide black exterior banding lines: one just below the rim and the second several centimeters lower, framing a white kaolin painted design. The interior again has a black banding line just below the rim, and then the bowl's interior layout begins.

The center interior of the bowl contains an icon not previously discussed. There is a wide ring which contains a large dot. This is the glyph for "something there" or "something held in one place" (see figure 8 and the sign language gesture in figure 9.) This is a fairly straightforward glyph, however,

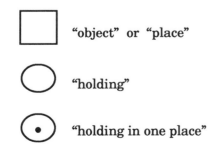

☐ "object" or "place"

◯ "holding"

⊙ "holding in one place"

Figure 8. Glyph showing "holding in one place" (From Martineau 1973).

the ring and dot combination could also be a variation of the "rain/water" icon. Meso-American and Casas Grandes examples often use a large circle and dot glyph for "rain/water" and in view of the fact that the entire remainder of this bowl is "rain/water" and related icons, there is a strong possibility that the center circle is also a large "rain/water" glyph.

This center ring and dot glyph is also ticked along the edges with "rain/water" symbols. This ticking or dotting to indicate "wet" or "water" is a common technique and has been observed on several petroglyphic examples.

Also on the interior of SW1013, just below the internal black banding line which is just below the rim, there is a series of white "cloud" symbols with "wind" extensions. In the curl of these "wind" icons and following along the edge of the "cloud" icons there are greenish colored "rain/water" dots. The combined icons symbolize the "clouds and wind bring the rain".

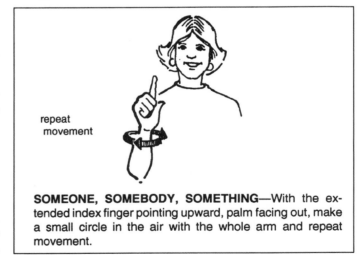

repeat movement

SOMEONE, SOMEBODY, SOMETHING—With the extended index finger pointing upward, palm facing out, make a small circle in the air with the whole arm and repeat movement.

Figure 9. American sign language gesture for "something" (From Costello 1983).

On the exterior of vessel SW1013, framed by the black banding lines, there is a series of horizontal parallel lines executed with white kaolin paint that run entirely around the bowl. In between these horizontal lines there is a series of white dots, a sequential diagonal pattern from the top edge to the bottom. This dot pattern is in pairs and there are five pairs in all. This has the appearance of notes on a musical scale. The two icons used are the "earth/land", i.e. the parallel lines, and "rain" as represented by the white dots. The combined meaning is clearly "rain falling to the earth". Color may be significant in the case of this combined glyph. Both the "water" dots and the "earth/land" lines are executed in white paint. This may be still another form of determinative, indicating that you read both glyphs together.

Because of the abundance of "rain/water" icons on this bowl, it was possible to identify not only several previously unknown "rain/water" glyphs, but also specific combinations of glyphs, such as the "rain falling to the earth" and confirming others like the ticking used to indicate "wet/water". Vessel SW1013 is virtually a synonym thesaurus of "rain/water" glyphs and their usage.

Photo 9. Vessel Pi5
"Two Pueblos Divided By War"

This bowl is a classic Gila Polychrome dating A.D. 1200-1450 and this falls well within the White Mountain Redwares icon temporal limits. This vessel was excavated south of the Mogollon Rim, and south of Raven Site Ruin. The Salado Polychromes are believed to have been influenced by the White Mountain Redwares (Steen 1966), and the iconography found on both pottery types is remarkably similar. The Gila Polychromes often demonstrate icons combined to form an overall vessel meaning. The Gila Polychromes are believed to be ancestral to Tonto Polychromes and the Tonto Polychromes often appear with recognizable motifs, but any coherent combination of icons seems to be absent. It could well be that by the time Tonto Polychromes were being produced by the Salado Indians to the south, iconography use on pottery was on the decline, just as coherent symbols were no longer being produced in the White Mountains area to the north after A.D. 1450. Many of the Gila Polychromes are difficult to translate because there are so many symbols present, and our known icon vocabulary is so limited. Also, many of the icons are slightly altered, often reduced from their original White Mountains prototypes and they are consequently often difficult to recognize.

Vessel Pi5 is a deep bowl with a flared rim. This form is typically Gila and is diagnostic of the type. The exterior is red with slight fire clouding and the temper is sand/sherd with some mica, also typical of the type. The interior is black on white and is boldly decorated.

Around the inside rim of the bowl are three parallel wavy lines. These lines are often found encompassing the rim of Gila Polychrome bowls. There are typically two lines, although three are

not uncommon. These wavy lines resemble known icons and could represent "water", "river", or "lightning", although there is so far no strong supportive evidence, and they remain to be translated.

On the interior side of the set of wavy lines, there is a wide solid black band which separates the three wavy lines from the bottom of the vessel, a common Gila Polychrome treatment. The solid black band is broken once. This "spirit break" has been explained as a passageway for the "spirit" of the vessel to gain its freedom. It has been compared to the ritual "killing" of mortuary offerings among the Hohokam and the "kill hole" found on Mimbres vessels interred with their dead (Fewkes 1895, Haury 1978, Moulard 1984). It is called the "onane" in Zuni, a road to life, a way to emerge from the sipapu. Other forms of ceremonial vessel "kills" are rim notching and deliberate rim mutilation. This "spirit band" or "spirit break" can be found on a variety of pottery types within our temporal frame, i.e. A.D. 1200-1450 both in the White Mountains area, and the Salado area to the south.

Filling the bottom of vessel Pi5 is the main theme of the bowl. A large "war" symbol in positive black crosses the pattern field. This "war" symbol has on each "arrow point" half a negative white circle with a cross in black at center. This circle with a cross is a reduced version of the "divided" icon. The White Mountain icon meaning "divided" would also display four dots, one within each quarter of the divided circle, representing "something divided" (see figure 10). The example here lacks the dots. The use of reduced icons is typical of the Gila Polychromes and often creates difficulty in translation.

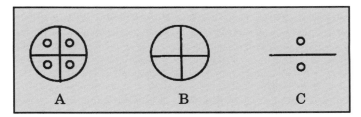

Figure 10. The icon for "divided" is formed by a circle or square (in the case of property) with a cross at center. The White Mountains icon includes dots (A) meaning "something divided", the Gila variety (B) is a reduced form as seen on vessel Pi5. The similarity to our modern icon is shown in (C).

Opposite the "divided" and "war" icons are two opposing "pueblo" symbols. These "pueblo" icons contain all of the elements common to the "pueblo" glyph. There is the "hill" icon, complete with "earth/land" symbols. The interlocked terraced units in the center of the glyph create the "geographical place" icon, and they also represent "house/marriage." A single "house/marriage" symbol is often used in the "pueblo" icon, instead of the multiple form. The "pueblo" icon when found on the White Mountain Redwares typically has more than one pair of interlocked terraced units, but the remainder of the iconographic combination is identical to White Mountains examples.

The only additional information presented on this vessel is the terracing on the outside of the "hill/mountain" symbol. This terracing on "hill/mountain" icons is not uncommon and is found on many White Mountain examples. This terracing is also found on "cloud" icons and the representation could broadly be translated "heaped up". The inclusion of the "earth/land" parallel lines confirms this representation as "hill/mountain" and not "cloud".

Although there is no indication by the position of the icons as to which symbol should be read first, second or third, etc., the positioning of the icons in relation to each other does provide information to aid in the vessel's translation. Relative icon positioning is critical in this form of glyph translation. The "war" icon "divides", i.e. separates the "pueblo" icons in the pattern. This is reenforced by the "divided" icon included in the "war" motif. This is an excellent example of a "key sign" or "determinative" as is found in the iconography of the prehistoric Southwest.

Another vessel with the same depiction as Vessel Pi5 has recently been discovered in the White Mountains area. Now, with both vessels for comparison, new symbol information has been discovered. The circle/cross "divided" icon may, in fact, be a clan or totem icon. The translation of Vessel Pi5 may be a warrior emblem defending the pueblo. The A, B, A, B layouts of vessel Pi5 and the newly discovered vessel are very similar to clan and totem emblems found on shield representations.

Photo 10. Vessel SW1008
"Determined Man"

This bowl is an example of an underfired St. Johns Polychrome dating A.D. 1175-1300. With the exception of the glyph in the center interior of the bowl, the remainder of the design layout is most likely aesthetic with no meaningful icon use. Isolated glyphs reveal far less information than those in combination, except to establish that the glyph was utilized during the temporal period of the pottery type's production.

The glyph at the bowl's center is that of a male anthropomorph. The distinction between male figures and those which may represent lizards is discussed in the icon section "lizard/man". This form of anthropomorphic figure is well represented on both prehistoric rock art and pottery from the Southwest.

The only other icon use on this vessel is the positioning of the arms and legs of this figure. Both arms and both legs are set at an extremely emphasized stance. They form rigid right angles to the body. This sharp cornered right angle symbol created by the arms and legs represents "will not be turned away", i.e. "determined" (Martineau 1973). For a discussion of this "will not be turned away" icon, see the vessel translation of SW1391a.

Photo 11. Vessel SW1391a
"The Thunderbird Brings Rain to the Pueblo"

This bowl is another fine example of a Fourmile Polychrome and it exhibits many icons in combina-

(Continued on page 41)

The vessels depicted on the following pages are from the White Mountain Archaeological Collection at St. Johns, Arizona.

TALKING POTS
Vessel Translations

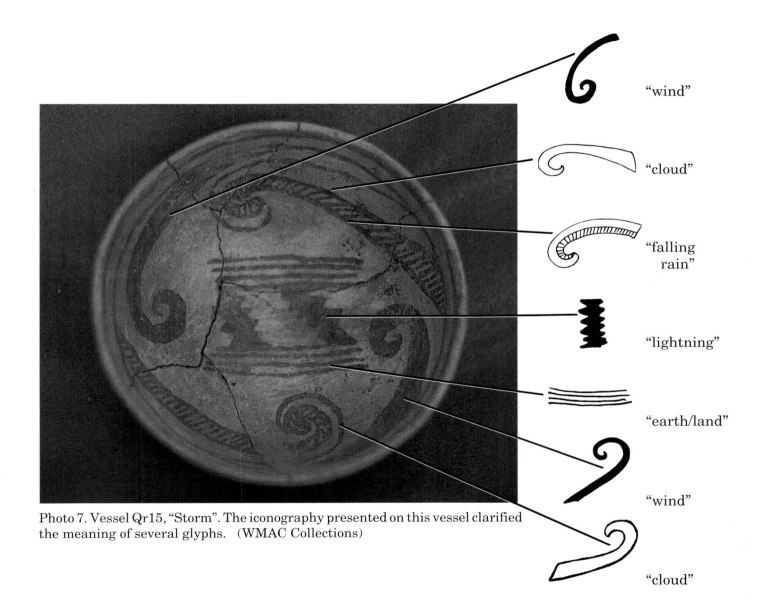

"wind"

"cloud"

"falling
rain"

"lightning"

"earth/land"

"wind"

"cloud"

Photo 7. Vessel Qr15, "Storm". The iconography presented on this vessel clarified
the meaning of several glyphs.   (WMAC Collections)

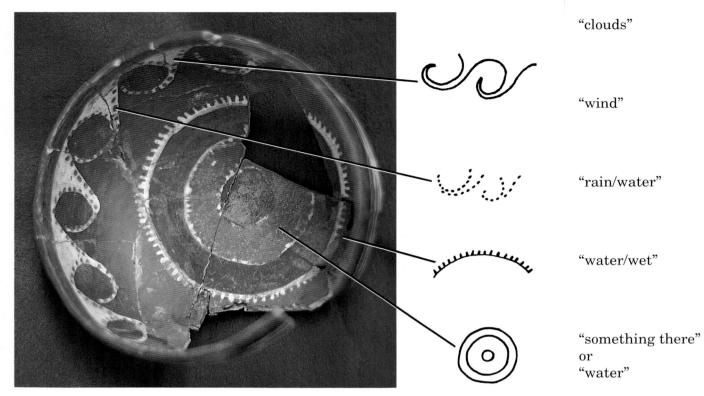

"clouds"

"wind"

"rain/water"

"water/wet"

"something there"
or
"water"

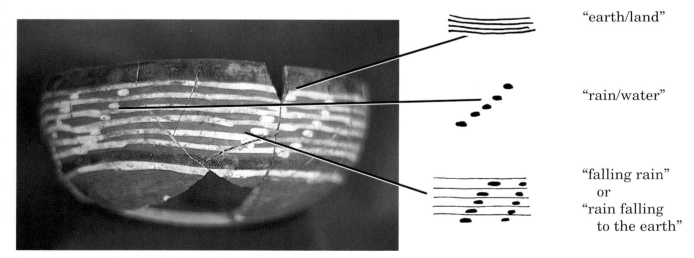

"earth/land"

"rain/water"

"falling rain"
    or
"rain falling
    to the earth"

Photo 8 and 8a. Vessel SW1013. "With the Rains, There is Something in Your Bowl." This small bowl illustrates at least three individual icons for "water/rain/wet" and even "falling rain." (WMAC Collections)

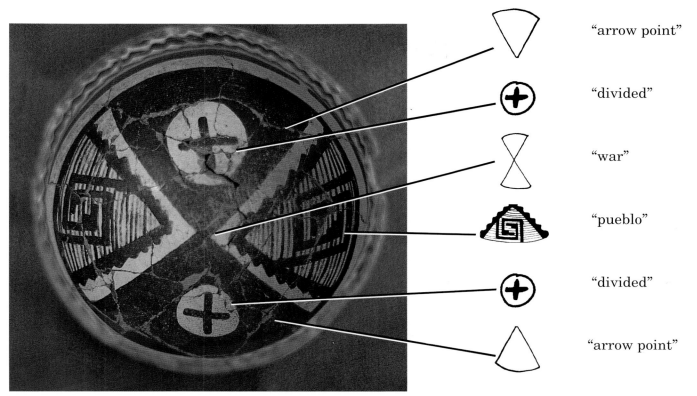

"arrow point"

"divided"

"war"

"pueblo"

"divided"

"arrow point"

Photo 9. Vessel Pi5. "Two Pueblos Divided By War". This vessel illustrates the importance of icon positioning. This positioning constitutes a "key sign" or determinative. (WMAC Collections)

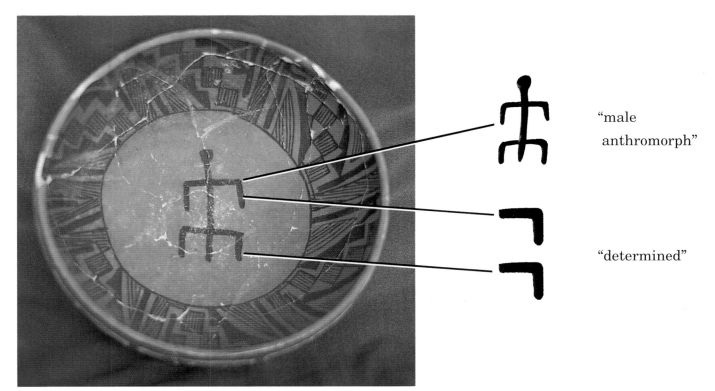

"male anthromorph"

"determined"

Photo 10. Vessel SW1008. "Determined Man." This anthropomorphic form is more commonly found pecked into the abundant petroglyphs of the Southwest. This representation says disappointingly little, except to reenforce the comparison between the use of iconography on both medias. (WMAC Collections)

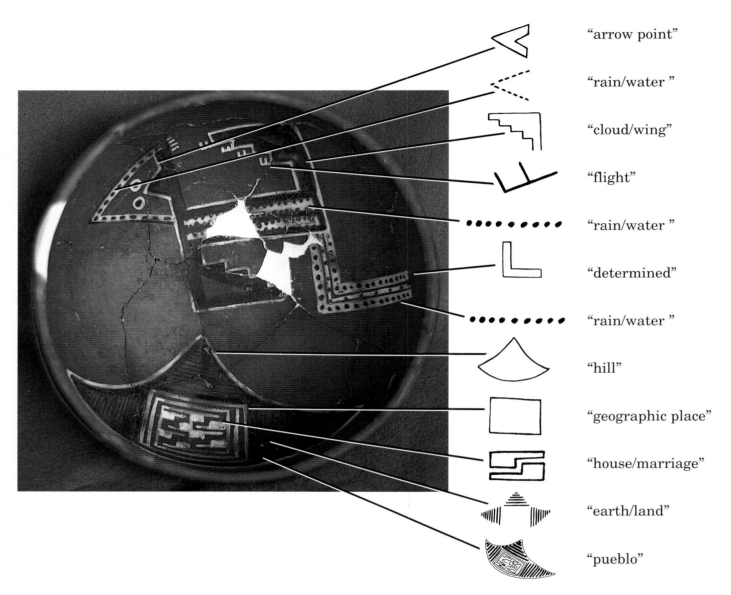

"arrow point"

"rain/water "

"cloud/wing"

"flight"

"rain/water "

"determined"

"rain/water "

"hill"

"geographic place"

"house/marriage"

"earth/land"

"pueblo"

Photo 11. Vessel SW1391a. "The Thunderbird Brings Rain to the Pueblo." This vessel elucidates a legend that was well known prehistorically, but the story has been lost over the centuries. Clearly exhibiting the height of the ceramic technology in the White Mountains region, the bowl also demonstrates iconographic combinations that hint at the very beginnings of a written language. (WMAC Collections)

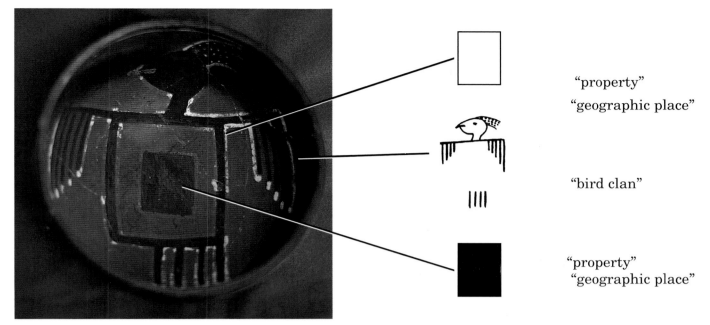

Photo 12. Vessel SW1501. "Property of the Bird Clan." Point of Pines Polychrome dating A.D. 1400-1500. This vessel combines the square geographical place icon with the attributes of a bird. It identifies property, and possession. The bowl was produced after the Fourmile Polychrome potters (see vessels SW1391a, SW1013, SW1011, SW305, and Pi2) had left Raven Site Ruin and moved north to Homolovi. It is a poor copy of a pottery tradition that was lost after A.D. 1380 in the White Mountains. (WMAC Collections).

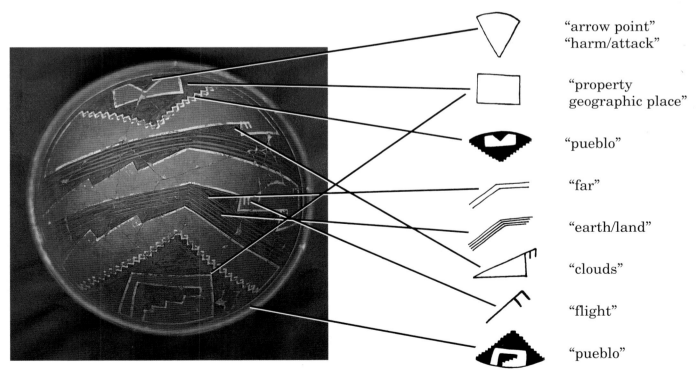

Photo 13. Vessel Pi2. "Far, Far Away, Across the Land and Under the Clouds, There are Two Villages, One is Large, One is Small, The Small Village is Under Attack." This is a fine example of a Fourmile Polychrome bowl which was produced at the height of the ceramic technology in the White Mountains area. The two "pueblo" glyphs on this vessel have been reduced and retain only the "hill" and "geographic place" icons. However, other information has been added within the glyphs to describe what is happening at each village. (WMAC Collections).

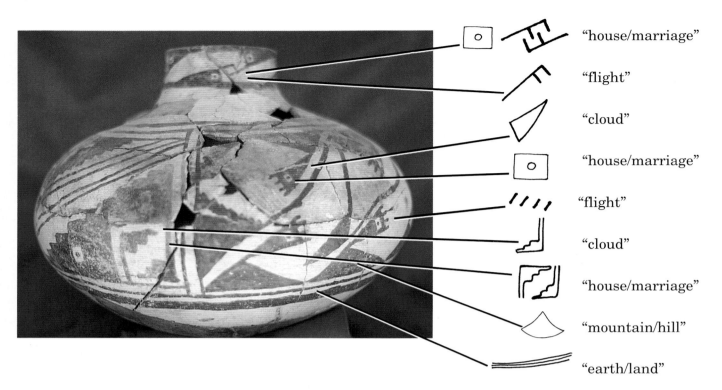

"house/marriage"

"flight"

"cloud"

"house/marriage"

"flight"

"cloud"

"house/marriage"

"mountain/hill"

"earth/land"

Photo 14. Vessel SW1509. "cloud/house." The author of this olla went to great lengths to convey a single idea. "Clouds" are clearly represented over "earth/land." The "clouds" are combined with "house/marriage" glyphs. The "house/marriage" icons are placed within the "cloud" icons. Even the "flight" icons on the "clouds" are interlocked to reiterate the "house/marriage" glyph. These "house/cloud" combinations are representations of the phratral organization "Patki". Vessel SW1509 verifies this clan group's influence at Raven Site between A.D. 1400 and possibly as late as the middle of the fifteenth century. (WMAC Collections).

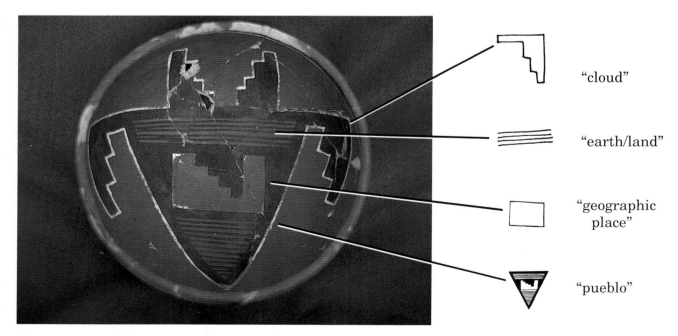

"cloud"

"earth/land"

"geographic place"

"pueblo"

Photo 16. Vessel SW305. "Thunderbird Pueblo." Fourmile Polychrome bowl with combined "thunderbird" and "pueblo" attributes. (WMAC Collections).

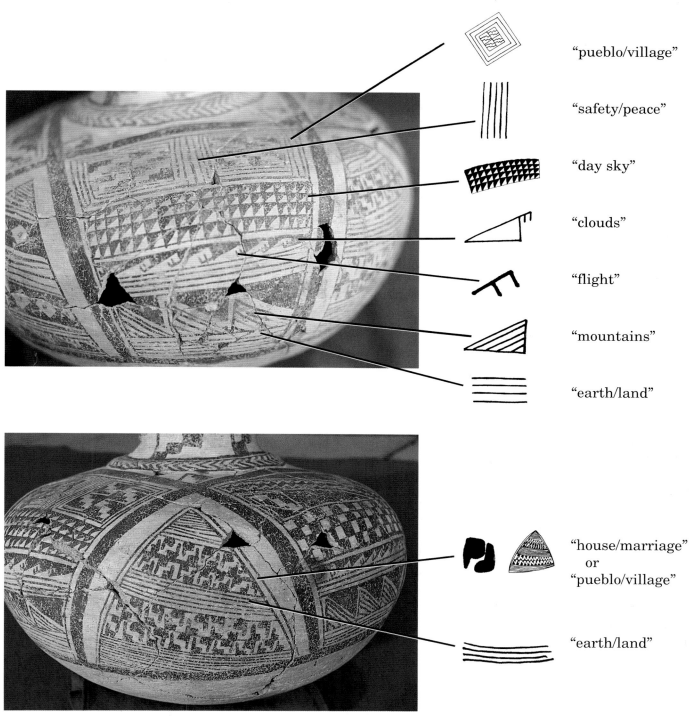

"pueblo/village"

"safety/peace"

"day sky"

"clouds"

"flight"

"mountains"

"earth/land"

"house/marriage"
or
"pueblo/village"

"earth/land"

Photo 18 and 18b. Olla SW1003. First main panel and supporting panel. Two villages at peace over a "day sky" with "clouds" in "flight" over "mountains" and "earth". The supportive panel reiterates the terracing of the "pueblo" and the "earth/land" symbols. (WMAC Collections)

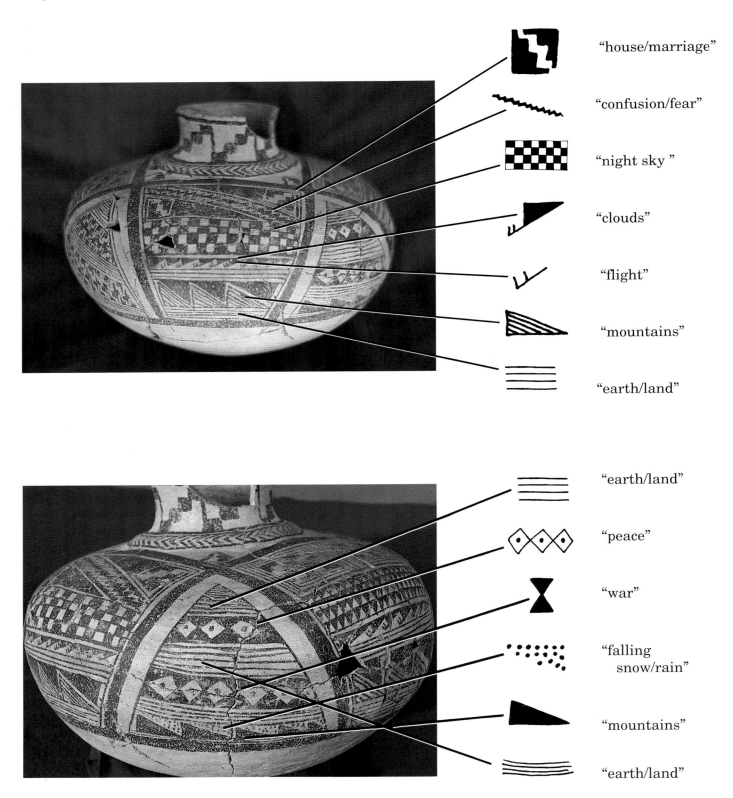

"house/marriage"

"confusion/fear"

"night sky"

"clouds"

"flight"

"mountains"

"earth/land"

"earth/land"

"peace"

"war"

"falling snow/rain"

"mountains"

"earth/land"

Photo 19. Olla SW1003. Second main panel and second supporting panel. Two houses in conflict over a "night sky" with "clouds" in "flight" over "mountains" and "earth/land"; and "war" and "peace", with "earth/land", "falling snow/rain" over "mountains" and "earth/land." (WMAC Collections)

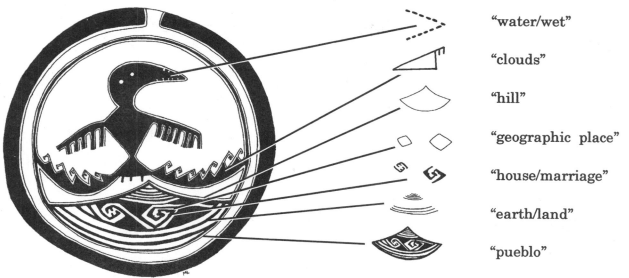

"water/wet"

"clouds"

"hill"

"geographic place"

"house/marriage"

"earth/land"

"pueblo"

Figure 11. Bowl from Sikyatki depicting the same narrative as vessel SW1391a. The thunderbird bringing the rain clouds to the village below. (Fewkes 1895)

tion to illustrate a prehistorically well known narrative. This vessel dates between A.D. 1325 and A.D. 1400 and possibly as late as A.D. 1450 (Carlson 1970) and it is a near twin to another vessel from the Sikyatki ceramic tradition, which occurred much further north. The migration of the Little Colorado people into the Hopi area is well documented (Fewkes 1895) and as demonstrated by this bowl, they took their stories with them. Photo 11 shows SW1391a and figure 11 shows the Sikyatki bowl. The similarities may at first be a little difficult to recognize until the analysis is complete.

On the interior of vessel SW1391a, there are two primary glyphs. The first is a thunderbird which is designed using several icons. The bird's head is an "arrow point" icon indicating strength or power. This symbol is reenforced by a second "arrow point" icon behind the first. This redundancy is common, several symbols with the same meaning used in combination to clarify the meaning. This redundancy may also be a phonetic element, repeating a symbol for emphasis. One is reminded of the Pima word "Hohokam" meaning "all used up". "Hokam" means "used up". The thunderbird's wings are one of the many "cloud" icons, i.e. the unilateral terraced unit. These "cloud" wings are complete with the icon for "flight" attached to each step of the terrace. Trailing in the air and attached behind the thunderbird is a most unusual glyph. This is a right angle figure, composed of three right angle forms, side by side, the two outer forms are wider than the central form, and all three contain greenish dots representing "water/rain". One trans-

lation for this right angled form is "determined/will not be turned away" as encountered on the rock art of the Southwest (see figure 12) (Martineau 1987). Another very probable translation is found in Athapaskan lore. In sandpainting depictions illustrating the Navajo Shooting Chant, this right angled glyph appears attached to the center of the bodies of buffalo. It is considered a symbol of restoration or strength (Newcomb and Reichard 1975). Furthermore, this symbol recurs in other sandpaintings, often trailing out of the posterior of animals very similar to the thunderbird in question, and it is described as a "rain streamer" (see figure 13.) Rain streamers are very similar to the Navajo depictions of rainbows although somewhat reduced in form. Translating this right angled glyph as a very early form of the rain streamer is probably correct. This is reenforced by the abundant dots representing water found throughout the form.

A variation of the line treatment of this glyph continues up from the right angled form into the body of the bird, as do the "rain/water" dots. This treatment of line into the body of the bird very much resembles the Zuni "heart lines" or "breath lines" found on modern depictions. The "rain/water" dots also border the "arrow point" head of this thunderbird. As graphic as this thunderbird is, and as recognizable as most of the icons are, there is still more that is being said than can be translated (note the trailing icon and the way the icon continues up into the body of the bird.)

The second primary glyph on the interior of vessel SW1391a is a beautiful example of the icon

Figure 12. Petroglyph showing the right angled "will not be turned away" symbol. The figure on the extreme left shows the rounded "turned away" symbol (From Martineau 1987).

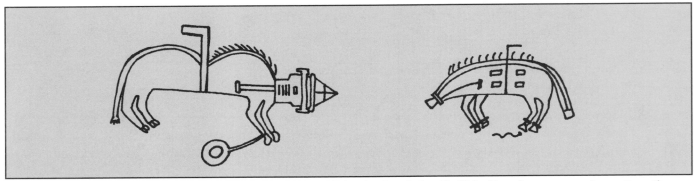

Figure 13. The crank like assemblage coming out of the back of the Buffalo People represents restoration or strength. Notice the similarity of this symbol and the rain streamer extending down the spine and out behind the animal on the right. These rain streamers are sometimes depicted extending out the back of animals and they are often right angled. They also often extend up into the body of the animal, as does our prehistoric example SW1391a. (From Newcomb and Reichard 1975).

"pueblo/village". A triangular "hill" symbol contains a square "property/geographic place" icon. Inside the square are four sets of interlocked terraced units each of which is one of the recognized symbols for "house/marriage". Surrounding the "house/marriage" icons and within the boundaries of the "hill" icon are parallel lines representing "earth/land". All of these symbols in combination create the icon for "pueblo/village". Other forms of the "pueblo/village" icon have since been discovered, but this vessel was instrumental in the initial recognition of this glyph. The number of icons used on this one vessel is impressive. The combined translation of all of the icons tells a story of a thunderbird "powerful, (arrow point head) determined, (trailing right angled glyph) who flies (cloud wings with flight icons) over the pueblo (many houses on a hill surrounded by crops) and brings rain (dots on the head, body, and trailing glyph) to the village.

Looking back at the Sikyatki example from J. W. Fewkes, it is not difficult to see the similarities

in the two bowls. There are differences in the icons, but the narrative is the same as the White Mountain example.

Photo 12. Vessel SW1501
"Property of the Bird Clan."

This bowl is a good example of a Point of Pines Polychrome. This is a prehistoric copy. It was produced after A.D. 1400 and after Fourmile Polychromes were no longer produced at Raven Site Ruin. Whoever crafted this bowl, saw and liked the Fourmile Polychrome vessels which were still present on the site, but they had no knowledge of how to produce them correctly. The design mimics the Fourmile Polychromes, but lacks the skill of execution found on the earlier ceramic tradition.

The center interior of this vessel exhibits a large bird with the "property/human created space" icon used to form the outline of the bird. A central solid black rectangle is contained within the larger rectangle which is used as the bird's body. The head of the bird is presented in profile with possibly both eyes facing forward although this is difficult to determine because of the poor condition of the bowl. At least one eye dot is present, and there appears to be other line work within the confines of the head of the bird. The top notch is executed in both black and white with white dots along the black lines. The wings are simple, straight black lines tapering from long to short as they near the body. The outer black lines are edged in white and the center lines are tipped in white paint. The representation of the tail is interesting in that it is not centered. This may have been an attempt to reenforce the idea that the bird is in profile. The exterior of the bowl is the interlocked "F" motif, again mimicking the earlier Fourmile Polychrome designs.

There is very little iconography presented on this bowl. The rectangular "property/geographic place" glyphs combined with the bird is most likely a clan symbol representing the property of the "bird clan" (see clan symbols), or the bowl may represent a place name, i.e. "bird pueblo". Other bowls excavated from the same habitation also exhibited very simple bird designs.

Photo 13. Vessel Pi2
"Far, Far Away, There are Two Villages, One is Large, One is Small, the Small Village is Under Attack."

Vessel Pi2 was excavated just south of Raven Site Ruin below the Mogollon Rim. The site consisted primarily of Salado Polychrome vessels. The White Mountain Redwares are believed to have influenced the Salado Polychromes to the south. Vessel Pi2 is a Fourmile Polychrome dating A.D. 1325-1400. It exhibits the normal black banding layout of the Fourmiles on both the interior and the exterior of the bowl. It doesn't have the bright red slip of the Raven Site Ruin Fourmiles and the iconography is far less graphic, possibly demonstrating the later Gila influence. With the appearance of the Gila Polychromes, the symbolism being used shows a marked reduction in form, not so much in the complexity of the combinations of icons, but just a simplification of the symbols being painted. This reduction of icon form is an indication that the symbols were widely recognized. There is no longer any need to include all of the details of a complex symbol for the symbol to be understood. Pi2 exhibits two "pueblo/village" glyphs that have been reduced to the two essential elements necessary for their recognition, the triangular "hill" symbol, and the square "property/geographic place"

symbol at center. These two signs are sufficient to create a glyph that means "pueblo/village" that is quickly and easily comprehensible. This is an indication that this glyph now held a wider distribution and use well outside of the immediate White Mountains area where it may have originated. Another good reason to reduce the icons—other than just making them easier to create— is that this reduction allows for other details to be included to the narrative, that the complete and complicated glyph would have prohibited. There would not have been room to put in all of the symbols to tell a more complex story if the artist must include "hill", "property/geographic place", four "house/marriage" glyphs, and "earth/land" icons just to relate the single meaning "pueblo/village". By eliminating all except the essential icons, the craftswoman has given herself more freedom, i.e. more blank area, to fill in with other details. This is very much the case with vessel Pi2.

On either side of the bowl's interior, there are two "pueblo/village" icons in reduced form. One is purposely larger than the other. Both "pueblo/village" glyphs contain other symbols at their centers which relate information about each village specifically. Both village icons also use a "hill" glyph which includes a terraced edge. This is not uncommon and could indicate a steeper/higher terrain such as a mountain. The larger village contains, at center, a single unilateral terraced unit. This unit in isolation represents "cloud" and in this case probably indicates a place name, i.e. "cloud pueblo".

The smaller "pueblo/village" glyph on the opposing side of the interior of the bowl shows an

FAR— The "A" hands are held together, thumbs pointing away from the body. The right hand moves straight ahead in a slight arc. The left hand does not move.

Figure 14. The American sign language gesture for "far." (From Sternberg 1987)

"arrow point" icon with the point of the arrow directed at the village. This indicates "causes harm" to the village, or the village is/has been attacked.

In between the two villages there are two sets of parallel lines, each set is slightly bent at the center. This glyph indicates "far away" (Martineau 1973) and it is identical to the American sign language gesture (see figure 14.) There are a great many more details included on this "far away" glyph. The parallel lines are the "earth/land" symbol. Above these there are the right angle solid triangle "cloud" icon complete with the icon for "flight". Here again, the repeated use of the same symbol could be a determinative which indicates emphasis.

The complete translation of vessel Pi2 reads, "Far, far away, across the land and under the clouds, there are two villages, one is large, and one is small. The small village is weaker, and under attack."

The moral of the story seems to be, "There's safety in numbers".

Photo 14. Olla SW1509

"Cloud House"

Vessel SW1509 is a Red-on-buff Pottery "unnamed" (Woodbury and Woodbury 1966). This ceramic type is a bit of a mystery. It was found in the south pueblo of Raven Site in association with a Pinnawa Glaze-on-white dating between A.D. 1350-1450 and a Kechipawan Polychrome dating

as late as A.D. 1375-1475. According to the Woodburys this ceramic type may have been introduced as late as the middle of the fifteenth century, which would mean that Raven Site may have been occupied beyond A. D. 1500.

There are basically two icons exhibited on vessel SW1509, "house/marriage" and "cloud". These are combined, the "house/marriage" icon found within the "cloud" icon, and the "cloud" icon is complete with the symbol for "flight" attached. This is repeated again and again. The "house/marriage" glyph is also formed, within a square "property/geographic place" symbol, by two interlocked unilateral terraced units with long vertical extensions. This again is the "house/marriage" glyph formed by what are probably "cloud" representations. On the neck of the olla, there are again "cloud" icons containing the "house/marriage" icons at center. The "cloud" icons in this case are complete with the icon for "flight" attached. This icon for "flight" is again the unilateral terraced unit, and this unit is again interlocked to create the "house/marriage" glyph.

The creator of this vessel went to great lengths to express the idea of "house/cloud".

The only other iconography presented are sets of parallel lines at the base of the olla, which represent the "earth/land" glyph. These rows of parallel lines are often used as the "earth/land" icon at the base of ollas which depict scenes. Another example is the Turkey in the Corn olla shown in

Vessel SW1509. This olla illustrates "clouds" and "houses" in combination, and this iconography probably represents the phratral organization, Patki, or, "cloud/house" clan.

photo 15. The "earth/land" parallel line glyph is clearly represented at the base of the corn plants. SW1509 uses the same glyph in the same way. Above the "earth/land" icon is a row of "mountain/hill" symbols above which the clouds are "flying".

This vessel contains other iconography that eludes interpretation. The vessel's poor condition and large hiatus limits translation, but the layout of the olla indicates that the icons used are in meaningful combination.*

This olla primarily translates "house cloud". This is reenforced repeatedly, and made clear by the "earth/land" glyph at the base of the olla and the "mountain/hill" glyphs just above.

The translation of vessel SW1509 was accomplished using the system of analysis discussed in the section "The Smoking Gun." This analysis relies upon the reduction of glyphs, i.e. separating the individual elemental icons from the larger collective units that are discovered in combination and have a "known" meaning. "Cloud" symbols are well established and easily recognized. The "house/marriage" icon was deduced from the larger and more complex glyph "pueblo/village". Throughout this study, this system has been employed. The translation of olla SW1509 eventually verified the validity of using such a system to translate the icons found on prehistoric Southwest pottery. Vessel SW1509 was brought into the lab, cleaned, analyzed and translated to read "house cloud" or "cloud-house". Initially, this did not reveal very much information, only that it was very important for the creator of this olla to repeatedly relate the "cloud-house" glyph.

While researching the early literature collected at the turn of the century by Fredrick W. Hodge, we made an exciting discovery (Hodge 1907-10). Hodge reports that the Hopi of the East Mesa villages had twelve principle phratries. The second of these phratral organizations is the Patki or the "house-cloud". Dependent clans include: Omauwu or "rain-cloud", Tanaka or "rainbow", Talawipiki or "lightning", Yoki or "rain" and other subgroups which encompass various aquatic animal symbols. The repeated "house-cloud" icons found on vessel SW1509 represent the signature or clan name of the second phratral group of the prehistoric Hopi. This is exciting for two reasons. First, this discovery helps verify that the system of translation which has been utilized to translate the vessels is basically sound, and second, this links the Hopi of the East Mesa villages to the prehistoric site under investigation where vessel SW1509 was excavated. If this connection between the Hopi phratral organization "house/cloud" and vessel SW1509 is correct, then this olla is physical evidence of the clan's existence as early as A.D. 1400. To further help this analysis, Fredrick W. Hodge also reports:

> "The Patki 'house/cloud' phratry includes a number of clans that came to the Hopi country from the south, and the now ruined villages along the Little Colorado River, are claimed by this people to have been their former homes." (Hodge 1907-10).

The ruin where vessel SW1509 was excavated is precisely where the Hopi claim the Patki clans originated.

This is the second instance where the icons discovered on the prehistoric pottery of Raven Site have established a link between the prehistoric and the protohistoric/historic North American Indians.

The first instance is the translation of vessel SW1391a from Raven Site, and "bird with double eyes" reported by J.W. Fewkes from the ruin of Sikyatki. Both bowls depict the same story, that of a powerful thunderbird bringing rain to the pueblo below. The two pottery types in this instance are spatially separate by about a hundred miles. This could very well establish a link between Raven Site Ruin and the Ruin of Sikyatki, just as vessel SW1509 may eventually aid in the study of prehistoric Hopi migrations from the south along the Little Colorado River to their present homes in the north.

Photo 16. Vessel SW305
"Thunderbird Pueblo"

This bowl is a classic Fourmile Polychrome dating A.D. 1325-1400. The black banding layout, both interior and exterior, is standard Fourmile, with two bands circling the exterior bordering a field of white designs in kaolin paint and the inte-

---

* During the 1992 field excavations at Raven Site, the remainder of this vessel was discovered in the south pueblo. Hopefully, after reconstruction, more icons will appear and complete the translation.

rior has a black banding line just below the rim. The entire vessel is slipped in red and both interior and exterior are decorated with both Black-on-white designs.

The interior center of this vessel contains a bold thunderbird designed using several icons. The body is a large "arrow point" glyph which is commonly used as the body of thunderbirds to indicate "strength" or "power". The head and wings of the thunderbird are the unilateral terraced unit which could be translated as "cloud", however, this glyph probably has several uses. Within the body of the thunderbird, there is the symbol for "property/geographic place" and contained within the square of this glyph there is another unilateral terraced unit similar to units which make up the head and wings of the thunderbird. The "property/geographic place" symbol, with the unilateral terraced unit contained within, has been observed on other examples both from the White Mountains and areas to the south, below the Mogollon Rim (see vessel Pi2). This combination of symbols probably translates simply "pueblo/village", the unilateral terraced unit simply representing the stone terracing of the buildings within the village. This would be another example of a reduced icon form. Village glyphs are usually shown with several "house/marriage" units within the "property/geographic place" symbol. Above and below the "property/geographic" place symbol there are parallel lines that represent "earth/land". The use of the "property/geographic place" glyph and the "earth/land" glyph in combination is strong evidence to translate the total image as a "pueblo/village" symbol. This is further supported by the overall image created by the triangle "arrow point" body of the thunderbird, which is not that dissimilar to the triangular "hill" glyph often seen with village representations.

The interior glyph of the "pueblo/village" forming the body of the thunderbird could be translated "thunderbird/village" and the total image could represent a place name. Another example of a "bird/place" symbol from Raven Site Ruin can be seen in the vessel translation of SW1501 (photo 12) which is translated as a clan symbol.

Photo 17. Vessel SW1011
"Siege"

This is a fine example of a Fourmile Polychrome bowl dating 1325-1400 (Carlson 1970)

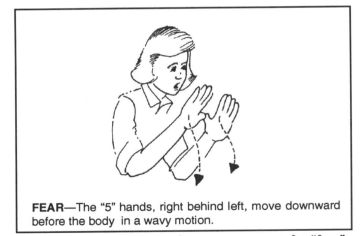

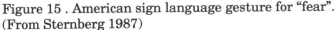
FEAR—The "5" hands, right behind left, move downward before the body in a wavy motion.

Figure 15 . American sign language gesture for "fear". (From Sternberg 1987)

and possibly to A.D. 1450 in the heart of the White Mountains. Fourmile Polychrome vessels seem to demonstrate the most frequent use of interrelated iconography, and the temporal period of their production is seen as the height of meaningful symbolism in the region. SW1011 is a deep bowl, slipped red on the interior and exterior and with both black paint of lead, copper and some manganese and white kaolin paint on all surfaces. The design layout is typical of the Fourmile Polychromes, with a wide black banding line used both on the interior of the bowl just below the rim, and on the exterior of the bowl below the rim, and then again lower to contain the field of design on the exterior.

The interior of vessel SW1011 demonstrates several icons in combination, including: "arrow point", "property/geographic place", "pueblo/village", "earth/land" and "confusion/fear".

The "arrow point" icons are four in all, and they surround a "pueblo" icon at the center of the bowl. The "arrow point" icons are pointing toward the "pueblo/village" icon, indicating "will cause harm".

The "pueblo/village" icon is set in a square, i.e. "property/human created space" and is surrounded by the "earth/land" icon, which is usually found in association with the "pueblo/village" glyph. The center of the "pueblo/village" symbol does not contain the usual interlocked terraced units. Instead there appears a zigzag symbol in negative, which resembles a "lightning" icon. In this instance, the zigzag symbol more likely reflects the idea of "confusion" or "fear". This symbol used in this way has been observed in Athapaskan mythology and it resembles the sign language gestures (see figure 15). The use of a different central symbol in the

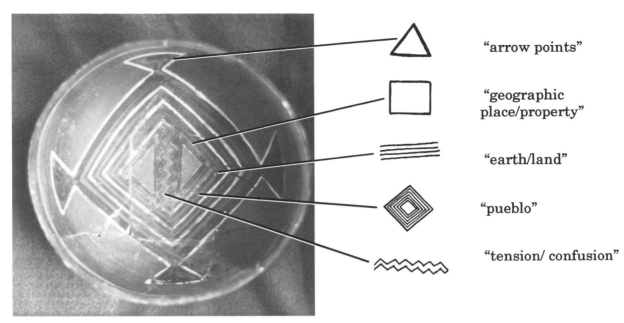

"arrow points"

"geographic place/property"

"earth/land"

"pueblo"

"tension/ confusion"

Photo 17. Vessel SW1011. "Siege." Fourmile Polychrome bowl with the "pueblo" icon surrounded by "arrow points". At the center of the "pueblo" is a zigzag glyph that represents "tension/confusion". (WMAC Collections).

"pueblo/village" icon, other than the usual interlocked terraced units, has also been observed on other "pueblo/village" examples.

When the icon is painted very small, often there will be three dots at center, representing three houses, i.e. "more than one" in the village. Single houses are often represented as a square with a dot at center. Finding a unique glyph at the center of a "pueblo/village" icon simply indicates "what's in the village", in this case "confusion/fear". The entire design of this bowl depicts the idea "siege". This is an elaborate example using several detailing symbols to clearly illustrate the theme.

Another example of a reduced "siege" icon can be seen in figure 16, a petroglyph from Galisteo Basin, New Mexico.

Photo 18 and 19. Olla SW1003
"Peaceful Villages and Houses in Conflict"

This olla is a fine example of complex iconography. This is a classic Tularosa Black-on-white vessel dating A.D. 1200-1300. The olla is laid out in eight panels divided by a wide black banding line. There are four pair of panels, i.e. each panel is mirrored on the opposite side of the olla. This banding line also isolates the neck area of the vessel. The neck is enclosed in an areola which is considered diagnostic of the Tularosa ollas. Because of the mirror image of each panel, there are

Figure 16. Petroglyph from Galisteo Basin, New Mexico showing the reduced form of the glyph for "siege" (From Martineau 1987).

four unique sections to be discussed. Of these four sections, two are the primary theme of the olla, and two are secondary supportive themes.

A primary panel and a secondary panel of SW1003 are shown in photo 18 and 18b. At the top of the panel, there are two "pueblo/village" glyphs. The parallel lines between the villages could depict "safety/peace" as mirrored by Athapaskan lore and symbols currently exhibited during the Hopi Snake Dance. These villages are positioned over a "day/sky" icon, then "clouds" with "flight" icons, and "earth/land" and "mountains". The glyph for "mountain/hill" on this olla is a fine example, complete with the "earth/land" symbol contained within the triangular borders.

The secondary panel shown in photo 18 and 18b is a supportive theme with redundant iconography in the form of interlocked terraced units in a banded layout with the "earth/land" glyph in between. The terraced units presented in this way are probably a variation of the "pueblo/village" symbol, and when the entire panel is viewed with this idea in mind, the overall triangular shape very much resembles the "pueblo/village" glyph encountered on other White Mountains examples.

The second primary panel and second supportive panel on vessel SW1003 is shown in photo 19. At the top of the second primary panel there are two "house/marriage" icons which oppose each other, divided by two "confusion/fear" zigzags. These are above a "night sky/Milky Way" glyph which is represented by the checkerboard. Below the "night sky" symbol there are "cloud" icons complete with "flight" icons again above the "earth/land" glyph and "mountains".

The second supportive panel of SW1003 is repetitive with "earth/land" bordering a series of "war" icons in negative and "peace" icons in positive. The peace icons are in positive, even though they are created by the white underlying color of the olla and not by the normally positive black paint, because they contain a dot at center which draws your eye to this glyph in the series first. The "war" symbol must be read between the "peace" symbol (see discussion of "war"). Below these icons and at the very bottom of the panel, there is a row of "mountain" icons with falling "snow/rain".

The overall theme of the olla is complex. There are two villages at peace over a day sky with flying clouds over the mountains and earth. There are two houses in conflict over the night sky with flying clouds over the mountains and earth. The supportive panels show houses or villages between the earth or land, and peace and war over the snow/rain falling to the earth in the mountains.

This vessel seems to be representing opposite ideas, depicting war and peace and day and night. It is interesting that the peaceful villages are depicted over the day sky and the night sky is associated with the houses in conflict. In pueblo mythology the war gods travel across the night sky via the Milky Way, which is depicted as the checkerboard. Most researchers agree with the translation of the checkerboard glyph as representing the Milky Way, or a starry sky. This olla exhibits a similar glyph on the panel opposite of the checkerboard. This similar glyph is also composed of a rectangular field divided into squares, however, the squares are bisected diagonally, half solid and half negative. This field of bisected squares look suspiciously like refracted sunlight. The idea is further supported by the appropriate sign language gesture for "day" (see "night/day" in the icon section). Because of the contrasting opposites this olla illustrates, it was instrumental in the translation of the "day/sky" glyph. No other examples of this possible "day/sky" glyph have so far been observed in context. It is offered here as a possibility and not a conclusion.

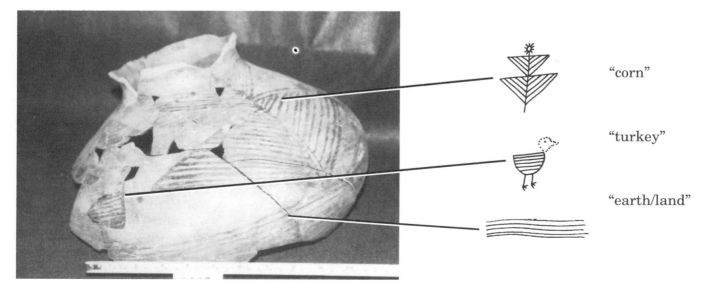

"corn"

"turkey"

"earth/land"

Photo 19a. Ga1b. "Turkey in the Corn". Although this olla has only three glyphs, the turkey, the corn plants and the "earth/land" glyph below the corn, it may reveal a great commonality of womankind. (WMAC Collections)

Photo 19a. Ga1b. "Turkey in the Corn".

This black on grey olla aided in the translation of the "earth/land" glyph and provided another graphic example of "corn". For many years, that was all of the information that the vessel provided. The corn patch is complete, including a turkey.

Recent Mayan excavations have discovered a small jar with a lid which displayed a glyph. This glyph has been translated "chocolate". Indeed, inside the jar the residue of prehistoric chocolate was found. The jar had been used to store chocolate for the family's use. Basic human behavior has not changed much in the last few thousand years. If you walk into any modern kitchen or workshop, you will easily discover a variety of containers with labels depicting their contents. Could olla Ga1b have contained something that is glyphically illustrated on its surface? In the room where the olla was excavated a great deal of prehistoric corn was also found. Metates and other corn grinding implements were excavated from the floor of the room. I jumped to the premature speculation that the olla had been used to store corn, because of the predominant "corn" glyphs. Seeking a biased second opinion, I displayed the olla to my wife. I told her the "prehistoric container label theory" and proudly announced that the olla most likely had been used as a corn storage container. Carol looked at the vessel and studied the glyphs and flatly told me that the vessel had not been used to store corn, but that the label clearly indicated it had been used to store the turkey food. Prehistoric peoples raised turkeys. They used the feathers, meat, eggs and bones. If you are raising turkeys, and have corn as primary cereal staple, and you are proficient in the grinding and preparation of corn, then it is not untenable that you would coarse grind some of this staple to feed the flock. Notice also that the neck of this olla is exactly sized to accommodate the removal of a handful of its contents. I further trust Carol's judgement because of her gender. Prehistorically, the women prepared the food, made the pottery and produced the glyphs on the pottery. The idea that a glyph displayed on a vessel might indicate the contents of the vessel is a common sense thing to look for when you are analyzing prehistoric icons. I picture a confused archaeologist a thousand years in the future, struggling to translate the illustrations found on the wrapper of a Snickers® bar.

The Icons

ARROW POINT △

The "arrow point" icon is most commonly utilized incorporated with other elements and is rarely seen in isolation. Its primary meaning is self evident, i.e. to cause harm, inflict injury, to hurt. This is the meaning assigned the icon when the point of the arrow is touching the object being injured or harmed. The "arrow point" icon also has more subtle translations. When the tip of the arrow is pointing away from the object under scrutiny the translation is "causing no harm". Often the "arrow point" icon is incorporated into a larger icon. This is frequently the case with thunderbirds. The "arrow point" icon is often the body of the bird, or the head. The implied meaning in this case is "strength" or "power", i.e. "the ability to cause harm". Thunderbirds are a common theme in prehistoric iconography on pottery, petroglyphs, and pictographs.

Photo 20 is a Fourmile Polychrome bowl dating A.D. 1325-1400 (Carlson 1970) illustrating a protectorate thunderbird with an "arrow point" head.

The idea of strength is redundantly exhibited with a second smaller "arrow point" within the first. The addition of eye dots completes the head of the bird. Thunderbirds are a common theme in the Southwest, and examples can be found over broad areas and executed in many media. The thunderbird was an important symbol; its function was to bring rain, as is evident by the "cloud" icon wings and frequent association with other water elements.

In figure 17, "arrow point" icons are abundant within the thunderbird petroglyphs.

Examples demonstrating the "arrow point" icon pointing toward another object, i.e. inflicting harm, are vessel SW1011, photo 21 and Pi2, photo 22. SW1011 shows four "arrow point" icons surrounding a "pueblo" icon. The vessel's overall translation is "siege", the "arrow point" icons representing the attacking forces. Vessel Pi2 again shows the "arrow point" icon, this time actually pointing into a "pueblo" icon inflicting harm or attack.

Protohistorically excellent examples of the "ar-

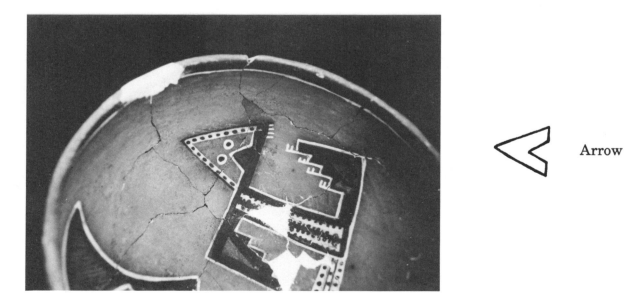

Arrow

Photo 20. SW1391a Fourmile Polychrome bowl dating A.D. 1325-1400 (Carlson 1970) showing a protectorate thunderbird with "arrow point" icon head. A second "arrow point" icon reenforces the first and eye dots complete the image. This redundancy may be a determinative device. The icon in this instance means "strength or power". (WMAC Collections)

Photo 21. SW1011 Fourmile Polychrome bowl with four "arrow point" icons surrounding a village. The overall meaning of the vessel is "siege". (WMAC Collections)

Photo 22. Vessel Pi2. Fourmile Polychrome vessel dating A.D. 1325-1400 (Carlson 1970) showing "arrow point" icon inflicting harm to a pueblo. (WMAC Collections)

Figure 17. Thunderbirds with "arrow point" icons throughout. Reproduced from petroglyphs from Mohave County, Arizona and Kane County, Utah (From Martineau 1987).

Figure 19. The Old Man of the Dalles. The "arrow point" icon on the old man's buttocks is pointing away, indicating "causing no harm". (From Seaman 1967).

Figure 18. Glyphs from Battiste Good's Winter Count showing several examples of the "arrow point" symbol inflicting injury and death. (From Mallery 1888-89).

Petroglyphs	Dakota	Ojibwa
△ Arrowhead	△ Arrow Point	△ Arrow Point

Delaware	Hopi	Aztec	Other
△ Arrow Point	△ Arrow Point	▲ Arrow Point	▲ Arrow Point (British Columbia)

Figure 20. Use of the arrow point icon by North American Indian tribes and the Aztec. (From Martineau 1987).

row point" symbol representing injury or death can be rediscovered among the winter counts of many tribes. Figure 18 reproduces several examples from Battiste Good's Winter Count as recorded by W. H Corbusier while stationed with the Dakotas in 1879 (Mallery 1888-89).

An excellent example of the "arrow point" icon shown pointing away from another figure and meaning "causing no harm" is represented in figure 19. The petroglyph shows an elderly beggar asking a lucky fisherman to share his catch. The "arrow point" icon on the buttocks of the old beggar is pointing away from the Old Man of the Dalles. This represents the idea that the catch will be shared and no harm will come to the beggar. The account is well documented ethnographically (Seaman 1967)

The "arrow point" icon is nearly universal. Examples of its use by the protohistoric North American Indians and Aztec is demonstrated in figure 20.

CLAN SYMBOLS

Clan symbols are included as part of the main body of the icon section, even though they are not individual icons. It is necessary to discuss these emblems here, because of their frequency not only on prehistoric Southwest pottery, but throughout the symbolism of the Southwest, be it on petroglyphs, pictographs or any other media. Clan symbols may well be the beginning of unit icon use to convey a wider meaning than simply the signatures of various phratral organizations. Clan symbols are composites, clusters of symbols, which are used to represent a family name or totem. They are used to identify property. They are signatures, emblems, and family coats of arms.

One clue that a group of icons may represent a clan symbol is the appearance of the square or rectangular glyph which is embellished to create an anthropomorphic or zoomorphic figure. The square or rectangle represents "property". The embellishment will contain the features which represent a particular emblem. The total symbol reads "this is so-and-so's property". The property which displays the signature/clan symbol may be a single vessel, or the signature/clan symbol may be found as a petroglyph on a boulder at the head of a canyon serving as a "no trespassing" marker (Kearns 1973). Clan symbols were also used to denote the location of communal lands (Turner 1963). Square and rectangular glyphs are often included in the signature/clan symbols found on pottery vessels. At Raven Site Ruin, during the excavation of rooms #20 and #21, vessels were discovered that exhibited bird icons in combination with other symbolic elements. These rooms were connected by a doorway and further analysis confirmed that these two rooms were inhabited contemporaneously. The bird motifs exhibited on the pottery from these rooms are most likely clan symbols. These bird motifs are very similar in design and they all occur on pottery of the same tradition and consequently the same temporal period (see photos 23, 24, 25, and 26). Interestingly, the use of the square or rectangle—

Chapter 3—The Icons

as included in the creation of clan symbols—may be the result of the inclusion of the idea of "house" in the combined clan glyph. The icon representing "house" consistently appears framed in a square or rectangle (see "house/marriage".) Clans are by their nature an extension of family groups or houses. To be included in a clan is to be identified with a particular "house". An example of this use of the "house" glyph included with other icons to represent a clan was discovered with the analysis of vessel SW1509. This vessel translates "house-cloud" or "cloud-house". The iconography is precise and repeated in various combinations (see vessel translation SW1509). In 1907, Fredrick W. Hodge recorded the twelve phratries of the Hopi of East Mesa. The second of these clan organizations was the Patki or "water-house" or "cloud-house". Dependent clans include Omauwu "rain cloud", Tanaka "rainbow", Talawipiki "lightning", Yoki "rain", and various aquatic animal clans. Furthermore, Hodge reports:

"The Patki (cloud-house) phratry includes a number of clans that came to the Hopi country from the south, and the now ruined villages along the Little Colorado River, and are claimed by this people to have been their former homes." (Hodge 1907-10).

Logistically, Raven Site Ruin is situated to the

Photo 23. Vessel SW1501 from room #21 excavated at Raven Site Ruin, showing the square "property" icon embellished with bird attributes which probably represent elements of a clan symbol. (WMAC Collections)

south of the East Mesa Hopi and along the Little Colorado River, and could very well be one of these prehistoric Hopi villages. Vessel SW1509 is an "unnamed Red-on-buff" (Woodbury and Woodbury 1966) which could date well into the fifteenth century. This vessel could be physical evidence of the "cloud-house" or Patki clan's existence at Raven Site just a few short years before Coronado marched from Mexico.

These signature emblems or clan symbols have been suggested to be the forerunners of the Chinese pictographic language (see figure 21), and are found as early as the fourth millennium B.C. carved on jade, ceramic and bronzes from the Lower Yangtze (Keightley 1989). Glyphs found in the Central Mexican codices are primarily personal names, places, and totems and the narration, for the most part, pictorial. Mayan glyphs abound with representations that are personal and place names (see figure 22). These often seem to be the prelude to the development of a more complex writing system. Even the basis of the writing system the West uses today may have evolved out of the desire to sign property. The earliest Greek texts seem to imply that the Greeks acquired the alphabet simply to establish ownership of objects and to show off writing skills (Senner 1989). The Minoan Crete as early as 1900-1400 B.C. used seal stones as signatures and the symbols employed were the prototypes of a later pictographic script (Stroud 1989).

The iconography discussed in this text seems to begin to appear in the early Tularosa phase of pottery development in the White Mountains area around A.D. 1200, with the appearance of clan symbols identified on black and white ollas. The use of iconography begins to expand to encompass more involved meanings than simply clan identification, with the advancement of pottery technology through the Fourmile Polychrome phase. The Fourmile Polychrome pottery of the White Mountains area appears to be the pinnacle of ceramic sophistication, terminating around the year A.D. 1400, at which time there appears to have been a period of abandonment, and shortly later, an influx of new arrivals from the south. The majority of iconography presented here has been observed on this Fourmile Polychrome material. This icon development appears to have begun with the use of clan symbols around A.D. 1200. The use of symbols for more involved representation continues to expand throughout the Fourmile phase of the 1300s, and then quickly degenerates after the year A.D. 1400, when the makers of this ceramic tradition migrated north.

It is important to notice that the beginning of this development around A.D. 1200 was very possibly the result of clans using symbols to identify themselves. This desire to graphically illustrate identity or create signatures seems to be the first step in the worldwide pattern in the development of a true writing system.

Other emblem forms that are encountered in the Southwest are circular representations with anthropomorphic features usually encountered as pictographs and petroglyphs. These usually appear as a circle, covered with icons, with a human head sticking above the top edge and two feet appearing below the bottom edge. Occasionally a full bodied anthropomorph will appear within a circle (see figure 23). Anderson (1971) suggests that these symbols stand for certain socioreligious institutions or affiliations. However, these representations have a greater similarity to "shield" glyphs encountered throughout the rock art of the Southwest. These "shield" representations may themselves contain the added iconography which would serve to represent the signature/clan emblem of the users (see figure 24).

How big these clans were, how many people they represent, how extended the family was, is not known. These signature emblems could be the mark of a single individual, or they could be as inclusive as representing an entire pueblo, or region.

Protohistoric examples of North American Indian signatures created by pictographically combining symbol elements can be found in Lone Dog's Winter Count for 1811-12 in the Dakota's census

Figure 21. Bird and sun motifs depicting ownership. Early Chinese. (From Wu 1985).

Photo 24. SW1494. Zuni vitreous glaze bowl showing bird motif which probably represents a clan symbol. From room #21, Raven Site Ruin. (WMAC Collections)

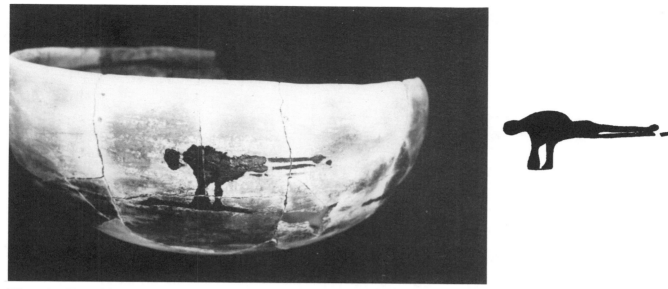

Photo 25. Vessel SW1390a, from the same habitation as SW1494 with a very similar bird motif. (WMAC Collections)

Photo 26. SW1383a. Zuni vitreous glaze bowl from the same habitation as vessels shown in photo 24 and 25, exhibiting a similar bird motif in a very stylized opposing form. (WMAC Collections)

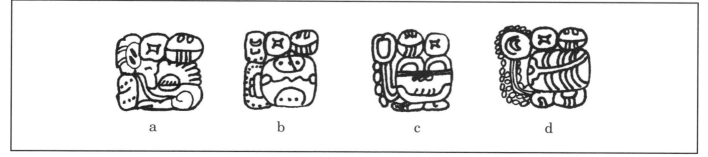

Figure 22. Mayan emblem glyphs (a) Palenque, (b) a second variety from Palenque, (c) Yaxchilan, (d) Quirigua. These glyphs represent place names (From Lounsbury 89).

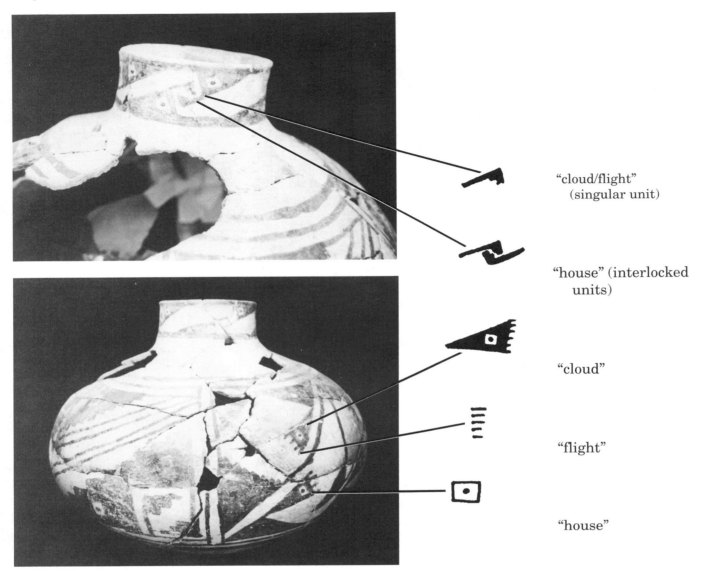

"cloud/flight"
(singular unit)

"house" (interlocked
units)

"cloud"

"flight"

"house"

Photo 26a and 26b. Olla SW1509. This vessel illustrates two glyphs, "house" and "clouds" which are deliberately combined. This "cloud/house" symbol may well be a clan name or phratral organization from the prehistoric Hopi dating well into the fifteenth century. (WMAC Collections)

Figure 23. Shield glyphs from the Tsegi Canyon drainage. The icons represented on the shield may be signature/clan names. (From Schaafsma 1980).

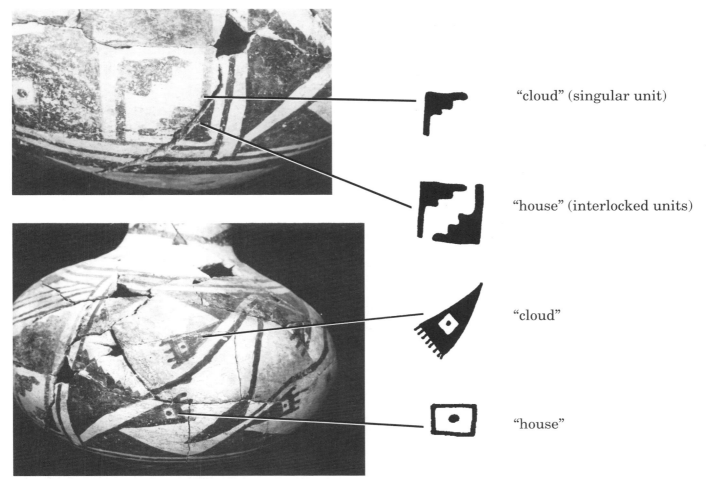

"cloud" (singular unit)

"house" (interlocked units)

"cloud"

"house"

Photos 26c and 26d. Olla SW1509. The terraced units in isolation represent the "cloud" icon. When interlocked, they create the "house/marriage" glyph, i.e. "cloud/house". (WMAC Collections)

Montana Texas New Mexico Nevada Canada

Figure 24. Shield representations from across North America and Canada. (From Martineau 1987).

Horned-Horse Grasp Four-Crows Female-Elk-Boy

Figure 25. Personal names from the Dakota census records showing realistic animals in combination with other icons. (From Mallery 1879-80).

records (Mallery 1888-89) (see figure 25). These examples usually combine animal forms such as "eagle/bear" or combine an animal with another element, a number or special feature such as "four crows". It is interesting to notice that these individual signatures do not include the square or rectangular "house" icon. Individual signatures and a clan symbol are difficult to differentiate from a modern perspective. Both mix symbols to pictographically represent a name, be it for one individual or many. Consequentially, the known protohistoric signatures are excellent clues to help identify the composite nature of the prehistoric clan symbols.

CLOUDS

The prehistoric icon for "cloud" is abundant on pottery and is usually incorporated with elements that represent characteristics inherent to clouds and other weather elements such as the icon for "flight", "rain/water", "snow", "wind" and "terraced/ heaped up". The icon is distinguished from its close cousin "wind" in that the "cloud" icon is almost always wider, i.e. it has more mass, the "wind" icon is narrow, wispy, and very curled (see "wind"). The "cloud" icon is often represented as a solid or negative triangle with no filler parallel lines. If the parallel lines are present, that is, the "earth/land" symbol, the icon would represent "mountain", the two being nearly identical visually. The "cloud" triangle representation often has the "flight" icon attached to the upper point or even the "wind" icon included as an extension. These extension icons are sometimes accompanied by water dots, the entire representation reading "clouds flying in the wind bringing rain". Vessel SW1330b, photo 27, is a Gila Polychrome A.D. 1300—possibly to 1600 A.D. (Cordell 1984) with "cloud" icons incorporated with the "flight" icon. This "cloud" form is often mistaken for a bear paw/track glyph. Vessel SW715, photo 28, is a Pinedale Black-on-white olla from Raven Site Ruin which illustrates the "cloud" icon again with the "flight" icon attached to the upper point of the triangle. QrPi21, photo 29, is a third example of the same combination exhibited on a Tonto Polychrome olla. Vessel SW1508, photo 30, another Tonto Polychrome, has the "cloud" icon complete with "wind" and "rain" symbols.

Another representation for "cloud" is a one-sided terraced symbol with the last step of the terrace slightly longer than the others. This icon is used as the wing on thunderbirds, which in this case is quite literal, meaning that thunderbirds have cloud wings. Vessel SW1391a, photo 31, a Fourmile Polychrome A.D. 1325-1400 (Carlson 1970) shows a thunderbird bringing rain to a pueblo.

This thunderbird has "cloud" icon wings in the one-sided terraced form complete with "flight" icons attached. Vessel SW305, photo 32, is another Fourmile Polychrome bowl depicting the thunderbird with the unilateral terrace "cloud" icon as wings. Figure 26 is reproduced from Fewkes 1895, *Sikyatki and its Pottery* and this bowl is nearly identical to SW1391a. The prehistoric migration of the Little Colorado people to the area and the introduction of their symbols (and probably their legends) is well documented (Fewkes 1895). The figure again shows a "bird bringing rain clouds to the pueblo below." The "cloud" icon is represented by solid triangles linked together with the upper point extended to include the icon for "flight". Fewkes also recognized the one-sided terrace form "cloud" icon and an example is presented in figure 27 (Fewkes 1895). This one sided terraced unit requires further discussion. It seems to be used frequently for cloud representations, but it is also used in pairs to produce icons with different meanings. Figure 28 is an example whereby two single sided "cloud" terraced units are paired to produce a lightning bolt in between. It should be noted that the potter of this vessel included the round semi-circles on the edges of the representation to avoid any possible confusion with the icon for "pueblo" or "house" or any of the other several combinations using the paired terraces that often occur.

A symmetrically terraced "cloud" icon can be found on Mimbres pottery (Moulard 1984). Caution should be exercised in using Mimbres pottery in icon interpretation. Often Mimbres pottery depicts specific people, animals, and events and ceremonies, not iconographic ideas. However, the example given here shows an anthropomorphic figure holding the Jornada style symbol for "cloud" in one hand (Schaafsma and Schaafsma, 1974) and "rainbow" in the other and his cap is again the "cloud" icon, i.e., the icons are deliberate, they are not real objects (unless perhaps ceremonial) or mistaken parts of the action depicted (see figure 29).

This double terraced form is exactly the same as a very universal icon meaning "heaped up/ high place/terraced/mountain", used by North American Indian groups including the Dakota and the Hopi (Martineau 1987). The similarities between "cloud" icons and "mountain" icons are obvious and has been previously discussed. To reiterate, solid or negative representations, i.e. without parallel hatchure lines, are "clouds", those with the hatchure line (the icon for "earth/land") are "mountains" (see "earth/land"). The anthromorph in figure 29 is holding a "cloud" icon which is solid and his cap icon is also lacking hatchure lines.

A third example rarely seen prehistorically, but one often depicted on katsina dancers both Hopi and Zuni, is the "triple domed cloud" complete with "falling rain".

There are dozens of other good examples of the "cloud" icon scattered throughout the literature, sufficient to say that it was a very important symbol to the inhabitants of the prehistoric Southwest. It is usually accompanied by rain symbols and other weather elements, and is associated with many ceremonies to insure good rain and consequentially good harvests. In the marginal environment of the Southwest, it's not surprising to see the "cloud" icon so profusely represented.

The modern American sign language gesture for "cloud" is presented in figure 30. The gesture reproduces the physical attributes of clouds as does the prehistoric icon (Costello 1985).

Figure 31 includes a description of the gesture used by the Cheyenne in 1879 which is virtually identical to the modern gesture and would most certainly be comprehended cross culturally.

Photo 27. Vessel SW1330b Gila Polychrome with triangle "cloud" icon complete with "flight" icon. (WMAC Collections)

Photo 28, SW715 Pinedale Black-on-white olla with "cloud" and "flight" icons. (WMAC Collections)

Photo 29. QrPi21, Tonto Polychrome olla with "cloud" and "flight" icons. (WMAC Collections)

Photo 30. SW1508, Tonto Polychrome vessel complete with "cloud", "wind" and "rain" icons. (WMAC Collections)

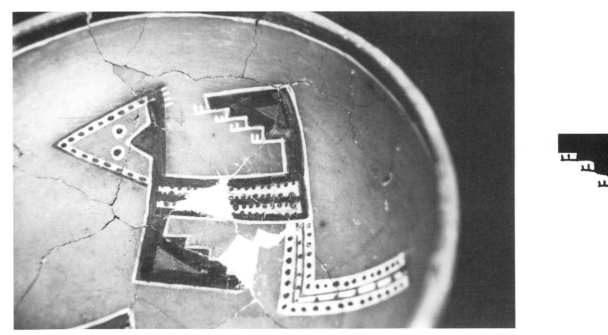

Photo 31. SW1391a Fourmile Polychrome bowl, thunderbird with "cloud" icon wings including "flight" icon extensions. (WMAC Collections)

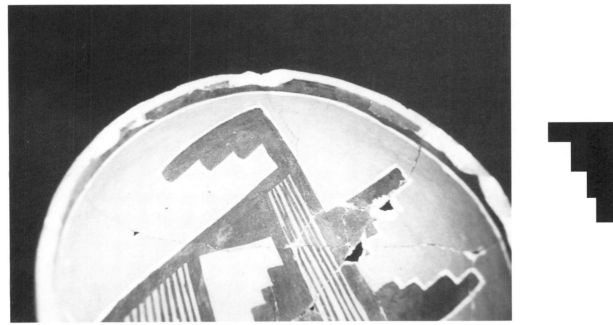

Photo 32. SW305 Fourmile Polychrome bowl depicting the thunderbird with unilateral terrace "cloud" icon as wings. (WMAC Collections)

Fig. 26. Sikyatki bowl, thunderbird bringing rain, the "cloud" icon is represented by linked triangles with "flight" icon attached.(From Fewkes 1895:271)

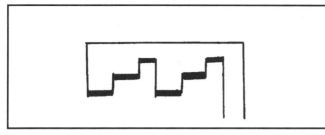

Fig. 27. Single sided terrace "cloud" icon. (From Fewkes 1895:257)

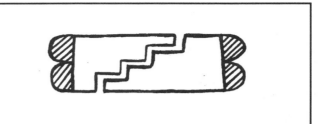

Fig. 28. Interlocked or paired single terrace units. This technique produces the symbol "lightning" between. Notice the domed units on each side which reenforce the cloud icon. (From Mallery 1889:702)

Figure 29. Classic Mimbres Black-on-white vessel. Anthropomorph holding double terraced Jornada "cloud" icon in left hand, "rainbow" in right, wearing a "cloud" icon cap. Raised arms and stance indicates "prayer" (Waters et al 1963). Probable translation of the vessel is "prayer/ praying for rain". (From Moulard 1984: plate 24)

CLOUD—With loose "claw" hands, palms forward above shoulder level, move hands in outward arcs ending with palms facing body.

Figure 30. Modern American sign language gesture for "cloud" visually representing the form of the "cloud" as does the prehistoric icon. (From Costello 1983)

A sign for cloud is as follows: Both hands partially closed, palms facing and near each other, brought up to level with or slightly above, but in front of the head; suddenly separated sidewise, describing a curve like a scallop; repeat for "many clouds ".

Figure 31. Description of sign language gesture for "cloud" used by the Cheyenne prior to 1879. (From Mallery 1879)

CORN

Icons that represent "corn" exist in two forms that have, so far, been identified. The most obvious glyph is readily seen in Athapaskan petroglyphs showing "corn" as a very realistic symbol complete with stalk, ears, leaves and tassels (see figure 32).

Figure 32. Athapaskan petroglyph with realistic "corn" symbol. (From Schaafsma 1980)

· This realistic depiction is not unknown on prehistoric pottery examples from the Southwest. Photo 33 shows olla Ga1b "Turkey in the Corn" with "corn" depicted in a slightly more abstract manner, but still easily recognizable.

Ceramic representations that depict the actual shape of an ear of corn can be found almost everywhere corn was used as a primary cereal grain. Throughout Meso-America ceramic representations can be found with the ear of corn shape, some even molded from the actual ear (see figure 34). It is not unusual to find prehistoric ceramics that mimic squash, gourds, or other vegetables. In the prehistoric Southwest, the "corn" shape became standardized into what some curators call the "submarine" vessel (see figure 35). This form first appeared around A.D. 500, with the first appearance of corn (Moulard 1984).

On a more symbolic level, the icon for "corn" is presented as a grid of squares or slight parallelo-

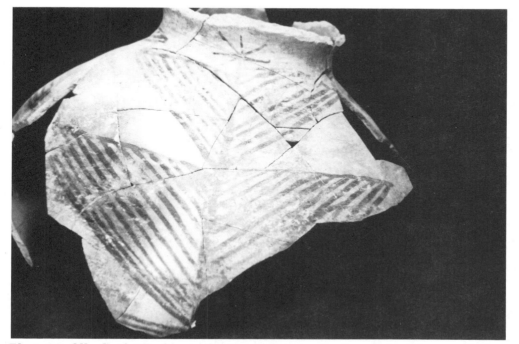

Photo 33. Olla Ga1b "Turkey in the Corn" showing the "corn" glyph in a realistic way. Notice the "earth/land" icon below the "corn". (WMAC Collections)

grams with dots at center. This iconographic representation is found in a variety of situations where corn is a theme. Figure 36 shows a Mimbres Black-on-white bowl with five Corn Maidens from A.D. 950-1150. The grid and dot "corn" icon is displayed on the heads of two of the maidens. The Corn Maidens are a prominent theme in modern Pueblo society. They are associated with agricultural fertility, death and resurrection. Corn Maidens are also identified with the different colored corns, and from the color designation there is often derived a directional significance. In mythology they are often described by their color designation. A very

similar depiction of the Corn Maidens has been discovered on a P IV mural from room two, wall six, at Kawaika-a at Hopi. Contemporary Hopi and Zuni corn effigies are often made with this grid dot "corn" pattern. Figure 37 is an example of a Reserve Black-on-white bowl demonstrating this grid/dot "corn" motif.

This grid and dot "corn" icon can be found on ceramic examples from all cultural groups in the prehistoric Southwest. This icon is often in isolation and is consequentially difficult to truly identify as "corn" and not just an aesthetically pleasing pattern.

One example of the grid and dot icon in the White Mountain Archaeological Centers collections from the Fremont culture in Utah includes a snake and bird effigy. In Pueblo mythology the water serpent is associated with the fertility of corn in the form of rain and lightning. The serpent on this vessel (see photo 34) not only has the grid and dot "corn" icon, but also the body of the snake is in the zigzag "lightning" icon form (see "lightning").

The icon for "corn" is presented in two ways. The first is an easily recognizable symbol of the entire corn plant. This appears both proto-historically and prehistorically on rock art and ceramics in the Southwest. The second icon for "corn" is more abstract. It consists of a grid and dot pattern and it is often found with other iconographic elements that are associated to corn mythology. Even in this more abstract presentation, it is not difficult to recognize the similarities between the grid and dot motif, and the actual corn cob and/or kernels.

Figure 34. Moche pottery from Peru's north coast. The rows of kernels are in alternating pairs, strong evidence that an actual ear of corn was probably used as a mold when this vessel was made. (From Gardner 1986)

Figure 35. Reserve Black-on-white corn effigy vessel, dating A.D. 950-1150 This form is not uncommon in Anasazi ceramics. (From Moulard 1984)

Figure 36. Classic Mimbres Black-on-white bowl showing five "Corn Maidens". The grid and dot "corn" icon appears on the head of two of the figures. (From Moulard 1984)

Figure 37. Reserve Black-on-white bowl dating A.D. 1250-1350 showing the grid/dot "corn" icon. (From Moulard 1984)

Photo 34. Fremont culture effigy vessel with serpent, bird and the "corn" icon in association. The serpent on this vessel also has "lightning" attributes. (WMAC Collections)

DEATH/DEAD

Although it is difficult to identify the icon for "death/dead" on a pottery vessel, it still deserves attention because of its direct comparative nature to the sign language gesture. The symbol for "death/dead" as identified on petroglyphs and proto-historic grave markers, is an upside down human or animal figure. It is not easily identifiable on a pottery vessel, because in the case of the interior of bowls, where the majority of icons on prehistoric pottery occur, it is not possible to tell from which direction to view the icons. If an olla or jar were excavated which displayed the icon, a viewing direction would be possible, and the icon could be identified. So far no such olla or jar has been found at Raven Site Ruin, and none to my knowledge exists. As I write this, I realize that as soon as this is printed and distributed, some private collector will undoubtedly produce a ceramic example that was previously unpublished, and I'm aquiver with anticipation.

Figure 38 is reproduced from Yarrow 1879-80, and illustrates proto-historic grave posts with the upside down figures indicating "death/dead".

Figure 39 is a petroglyphic panel from Rainy Lake, Ontario, Canada, which tells a tale of a canoe capsizing and one man drowned, as indicated by the upside down figure.

Other images exist among the pottery and petroglyphs that depict "death/dead", however, the inverted animal/human symbol is the most universal. Petroglyphs will often depict death by showing an anthromorph minus the head, or they will illustrate a successful hunt by drawing a realistic animal with an arrow through its heart. Figure 40 is a Mimbres vessel which depicts a decapitation. The victim is obviously illustrated as being deceased. Decapitations and cranes are a repeated theme on Mimbres ceramics.

There is one other possible "death/dead" icon which has often been observed on the Jornada style art (Schaafsma and Schaafsma 1974) of the prehistoric Southwest. Frequent on Mimbres vessels, Casas Grandes, and occasionally on other types, there appears a "death face" similar to depiction found in Mesoamerica. This Janus face is shown on the vessels illustrated in figures 41 and 42, and it is always shown with the gnashing teeth and triangular flesh-less nose of a skull. The nature of these Janus faces seem to relate to stories of death and often rebirth, and the presence of the Janus face may be a second true "death/dead" glyph.

Figure 43 illustrates the American sign language gesture for "death/dead" and the similarities to the prehistoric icon are remarkable.

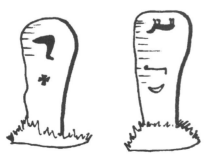

Figure 38. Protohistoric grave posts showing inverted animal figures indicating "death/dead". (From Yarrow 1879-80)

Figure 39. Petroglyph from Rainy Lake, Ontario, Canada, showing an inverted man indicating death. (From Martineau 1987)

Figure 40. Mimbres Black-on-white bowl showing decapitation. (From Brody 1977)

Figure 42. Casas Grandes Villa Ahumada Polychrome jar, dating A.D. 1205-1340 showing the Janus face. (From Moulard 1984)

Figure 41. Mimbres Black-on-white bowl dating A.D. 950-1150 showing two figures with Janus faces. These skull-like depictions could be a "death/dead" glyph. (From Moulard 1984)

DEATH, DEAD, DIE, EXPIRE, PERISH—Hold both flat hands to the front with the right palm facing up and the left palm facing down. Move both hands in an arc to the left while changing the hand positions so that the palms reverse direction.

Figure 43. The American sign language gesture for "death/dead". The similarities to the prehistoric icon are obvious. (From Butterworth and Flodin 1983)

EARTH/LAND

The icon for "earth" became apparent with the excavation of vessel SW1391a (see photo 35), a Fourmile bowl clearly showing a protectorate thunderbird flying over a pueblo bringing rain. The symbolism on the bowl illuminated several previously uncertain icons. Surrounding the pueblo on the mountain, there are illustrated rows or lines parallel to the pueblo on all sides. These look suspiciously like rows of irrigated cultigens. One is reminded of the "straight furrow" pattern used in quilting. With that possibility in mind, we reexamined several other vessels in an attempt to collaborate the possibility that these straight lines represented an "earth/land" icon. Many examples were found which illustrated the pueblo icon complete with the parallel lines.

Vessel SW1011 (see photo 36) shows the pueblo icon with the "earth/land" lines present. Vessel QrPi20 (see photo 37) is another example. SW1003 (see photo 38) again demonstrates this idea. There are several examples throughout the material held in the White Mountain Archaeological Center collections. In almost every case where the pueblo icon is illustrated, the crop lines around the pueblo are included. This is also the case when the icon for pueblo is carved as a petroglyph or painted as a pictograph, although there are fewer crop rows represented, possibly because of the difficulties due to the stone media (see figure 44 and 45).

The next step to the translation was to unravel an iconographic dilemma we had previously experienced. Many vessels illustrate right triangles, some with parallel lines like our crop lines, and some without. With the translation of the icon for "flight", part of the puzzle was solved. The triangles with the attached icon for "flight" are clouds. These never contain the parallel lines used to represent crops or "earth". These cloud triangles are usually solid, although sometimes in negative. Remember, this "cloud" representation is only one of many (see "Clouds" page 58). The triangles which include the parallel lines represent mountains, the parallel lines are "earth" and this combined with the triangle equals "mountain". So far, no right triangles which include the "earth/land/rows of cultigens"

icon have been discovered which counter this theory by also exhibiting an icon for "flight".

Also prevalent on many vessels are filler parallel lines. These could fall into the category of plaids and paisleys, i.e. just pretty designs, however, with the interpretation of the "earth" icon, it became necessary to take a second look.

Vessel Qr15 (see photo 39) clearly shows a violent thunderstorm complete with swirling wind and rain and lightning striking the earth. The earth is represented by parallel lines. This bowl originally caused confusion because there are parallel lines that appear to be both above and below the lightning which would seem to indicate that "earth" and "sky" were the same icon, both represented by the parallel lines. The idea that both "earth" and "sky" could share the same icon is not untenable. Upon closer examination of the vessel, the sky is clearly illustrated in the "wind" and "rain" icons around the rim. The double "earth/land" icons are on both sides of the lightning for the sake of symmetry.

There is one example of an icon found in the protohistoric literature which represents both "earth" and "sky". According to Frank H. Cushing, as recorded in the folktales of the Zuni Indians during the nineteenth century, the earth is represented by terraced units, and the sky is represented by inverted terraced units. This could also explain the abundance of these units found on prehistoric pottery. Often both are represented individually and interlocked, one including the "earth/land/ rows of cultigens" icon and one solid. The solid unit may, in fact, represent the "sky" (see "Basic Building Blocks").

Vessel SW1330b (see photo 40) has solid "clouds" complete with the "flight" icon and below these are parallel lines representing the "earth".

Vessel Pi2 (see photo 41) again has "cloud" icons with "flight" icons attached. These "clouds" are again flying over the "earth" which is represented by parallel lines. Vessel Ga1b (see photo 42) has the "earth/land" icon illustrated below the "corn" glyph.

Vessel SW1003 (see photos 43 and 45) illustrates a very involved combination of "earth/mountain/clouds", "earth/clouds", and "earth/clouds/rain". In all three combinations on this vessel, the "earth" is symbolized by parallel lines, the "mountains" by triangles filled with parallel lines, and the "clouds" are solid or negative triangles without parallel lines and with or without the "flight" icon.

An excellent example of Mexican pictographs for "cultivated soil" can be seen in figure 44 (Mallery 1879-80:382,383). These are clearly identical to the pottery icon.

The icon for "earth/land/rows of crops" is represented by parallel lines. This is not to say that all parallel lines on all vessels mean "earth". Some designs of this nature will fall into the plaid and paisley category, i.e. just attractive filler patterns.

The American sign language representation for "earth" is not relevant to the prehistoric icon. The problem lies in the fact that the modern sign demonstrates the earth rotating on its axis (Costello 1983:174). Prehistoric populations probably had no knowledge of the earth's axis or rotation and we should not expect an icon of this nature anymore than we could discover an icon for "rocket". However, the modern sign language gesture for "field/land", i.e. "earth" (Costello 1983:173), is an exact match, and gesturally demonstrates rows of crops (see figures 46 and 47).

Figure 44, Mexican pictograph for "cultivated soil, showing parallel lines representing crop rows. Notice the figure on the right showing vegetation. (From Mallery 1879-80:382-383)

Figure 45. Two reduced "pueblo/house" petroglyphs (depicting migration). Hovenweep, New Mexico (From Barnes 1982:241). Fewer "earth/land" lines are represented probably because of the difficult stone media.

Photo 35. Vessel 1391a Fourmile Polychrome A.D. 1325-1400 (Carlson 1970) protectorate bird flying over a "pueblo" surrounded by the "earth/land" glyph. (WMAC Collections)

Photo 36. Vessel SW1011 Fourmile Polychrome A.D. 1325-1400 (Carlson 1970) "siege" showing "pueblo" icon with the "earth/land" glyph. (WMAC Collections)

Photo 37. QrPi20 Vessel showing "pueblo" icon with "earth/land" (WMAC Collections)

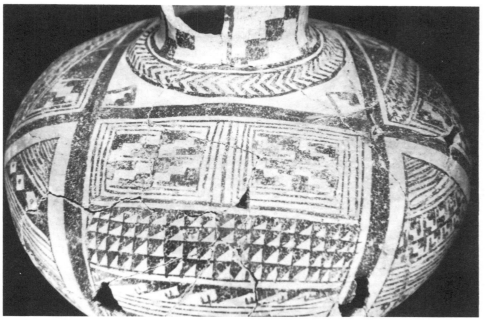

Photo 38. Vessel SW1003 Tularosa Black and White olla (Carlson 1970) showing two "pueblos" with the "earth/land" glyph. Excavated from Raven Site Ruin, Springerville, Arizona. (WMAC Collections)

Photo 39. Vessel Qr15 "Thunderstorm" showing "earth" as parallel lines. The "sky" is represented by the rim of the bowl with "wind" and "rain" icons. (WMAC Collections)

Photo 40. Vessel SW1330b Gila Polychrome A.D. 1300 + possibly produced as late as A.D. 1600 (Cordell 1984). Illustrates "clouds" with "flight" icon over "earth" represented by parallel lines. (WMAC Collections)

Photo 41. Vessel Pi2, Fourmile Polychrome, A.D. 1325-1400 (Carlson 1970) showing "clouds" with "flight" icon over "earth" icon represented by parallel lines. (WMAC Collections)

Photo 42. Vessel Ga1b, showing the "earth/land" icon as parallel lines below the corn plants. (WMAC Collections)

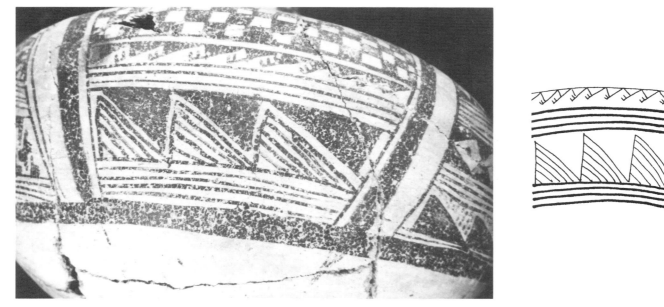

Photo 43. SW1003 Tularosa vessel, A.D. 1200-1300 (Carlson 1970) showing "earth", "mountain", "clouds". (WMAC Collections)

Photo 45. SW1003 showing "earth"," clouds" and "rain" or "snow". (WMAC Collections)

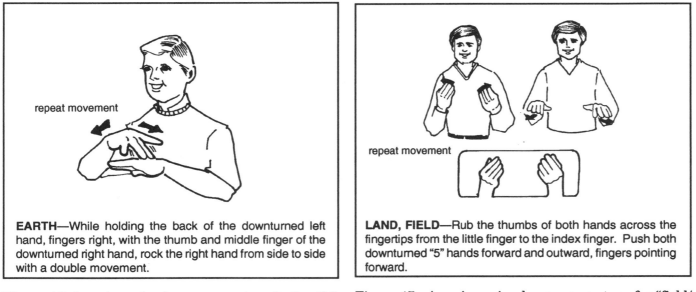

EARTH—While holding the back of the downturned left hand, fingers right, with the thumb and middle finger of the downturned right hand, rock the right hand from side to side with a double movement.

Figure 46. American sign language gesture for "earth". (From Costello 1983:174)

LAND, FIELD—Rub the thumbs of both hands across the fingertips from the little finger to the index finger. Push both downturned "5" hands forward and outward, fingers pointing forward.

Figure 47. American sign language gesture for "field/ land" i.e. "earth" demonstrating the flat land. (From Costello 1983:173)

FLYING/FLIGHT

The icon that represents the idea of "flying", "flight", "movement through the air", or the presence of a physical object in the position of the sky, "it can fly", "it is flying", is represented by the addition of short lines attached to the thing that is involved in flight. These consist of usually two or more, either positioned on the actual wing of the creature flying as in the case of a bird or butterfly, or the lines are attached to a short extension from the object, as is often the case with clouds. These short "flight" lines attached to the "cloud" icon help distinguish "clouds" from "mountains", the two being nearly visually identical both in reality and in iconography. The "mountain" icon also will contain the "earth/land" icon of parallel lines whereas the "cloud" icon will not. Clouds are a frequent theme in the iconography of the prehistoric Southwest. Clouds bring rain, and rain, i.e. water is the most critical single element for survival in this marginal environment (Cordell 1984:2).

It is possible that these short extensions could mean "movement" as is the case in the comic strips today where two lateral lines are used to represent the motion of a dog's tail or the vibrations resulting from a bang on the head. However, because these lines are attached to things that fly, and so far have not been observed on things that do not fly, it is a more positive assumption that they represent flight.

Figure 48 illustrates another butterfly with the "flight" extensions added to the wings. This vessel is a Kwakina Polychrome from the White Mountain area in Arizona.

Vessel SW1495 (see photo 46), has three butterflies around the edge of the rim, all three have the short extension lines that represent "flight". This vessel is of the Tularosa variety, dating from A.D. 1200-1300, and possibly longer in the heart of Zuni country (Carlson 1970:91).

Vessel SW1391a (see photo 47), shows a protectorate thunderbird flying over a pueblo. On the ends of the wings the short "flight" icon can be seen. This vessel is a classic Fourmile dating A.D. 1325-1400 (Carlson 1970:71).

Vessel Pi2 (see photo 48), is another Fourmile Polychrome vessel showing the "flight" icon on the ends of clouds.

Vessel SW715 (see photo 49), is a Black-on-white olla of the Pinedale variety dating A.D. 1300-1400 (Carlson 1970:94). Here again clouds are shown with the "flight" icon attached.

Vessel SW1003 (see photo 50) is another Tularosa, and again as with the Pinedale olla, this olla has the "flight" icon attached to the tips of clouds.

Very often birds are represented with what authors have called a "top-notch" on the head of the bird. This is usually represented by one or more short lines attached to the head. The idea that these lines are top-notches comes primarily from Hohokam ceramics which are quite graphic about the species of bird represented. In the case of the Hohokam material, the top-notches are painted to represent quail, which indeed they do (Haury 1978:232). To translate all lines attached to birds heads as quail top-notches is careless. All birds are not quail. Quite often these lines may be the "flight" icon simply attached to the head of the bird instead of to the wing.

The sign language representation for "to fly" is reproduced in figure 49 (Costello 1983:171), and clearly reenforces the use of the short lines or extensions to represent the idea of flight, the three fingers protruding being equivalent to the extensions. These probably evolved from the idea of "wing". Attach a wing, and you attach the idea of flight.

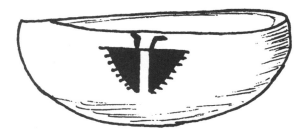

Figure 48. Kwakina Polychrome bowl from the White Mountains area, showing butterfly with the "flight" icon. (From Carlson 1970)

Photo 46. SW1495 Tularosa Black-on-white jar showing butterflies with the "flight" icon attached to the "wings". Vessel dates from A.D. 1200-1300 (Carlson 1970) (WMAC Collections)

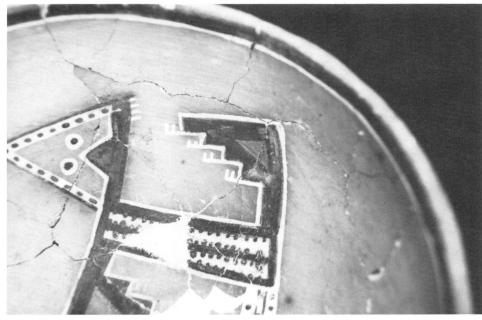

Photo 47. SW1391a Fourmile Polychrome bowl, A.D. 1325-1400 (Carlson 1970:91) showing "protectorate bird" with "flight" icon attached to the "wings". (WMAC Collections)

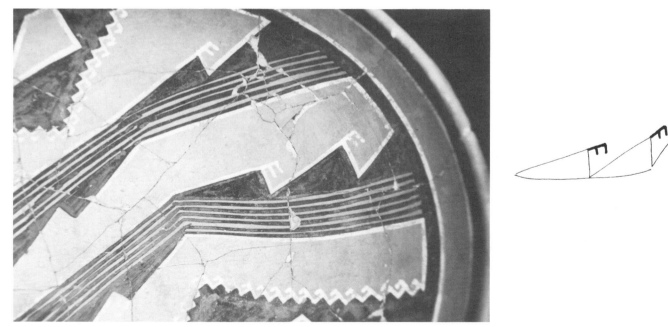

Photo 48. Pi2, Fourmile Polychrome vessel with "flight" icon attached to "clouds". (WMAC Collections)

Photo 49. SW715 Pinedale Black-on-white olla, dating A.D. 1300-1400 (Carlson 1970:94) with the "flight" icon attached to "clouds". (WMAC Collections)

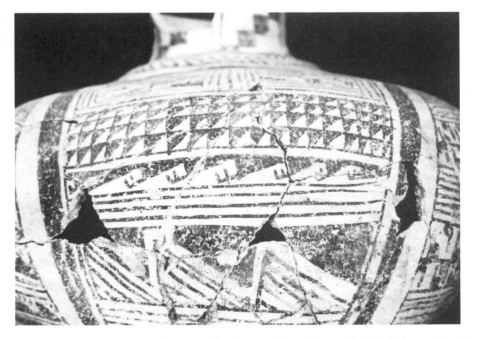

Photo 50. SW1003 Tularosa Black-on-white olla, with "flight" attached to "clouds". (WMAC Collections)

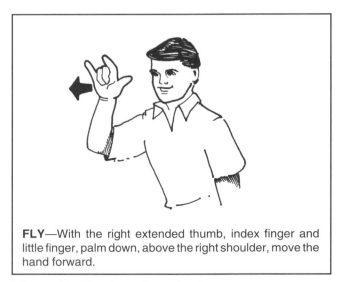

FLY—With the right extended thumb, index finger and little finger, palm down, above the right shoulder, move the hand forward.

Figure 49. The American sign language representation of "to fly", projecting fingers represent attached wings, attached wings represent flight. (From Costello 1983:171)

FOUR DIRECTIONS

The four cardinal directions have long been recognized as the swastika glyph. This phenomena is not isolated to the prehistoric American Southwest. The Aztec used the symbol to indicate "four directions" and the Chinese had the same glyph to represent "the four regions of space", the form representing the heavens in motion (Wilson 1894). The symbol has also been found on the prehistoric and proto-historic art work of the Eastern U.S. Photo 51 is an example of a Quapaw pottery jar dating from A.D. 1650-1750 (Hathcock 1983) from the White Mountain Archaeological Center 's collections exhibiting the swastika in a swirling design as if the "wind" icon had been modified. This swirling treatment is common on the pottery from the Mississippi River Valley from A.D. 1000-1650. The "four directions" symbol has also frequently appeared much earlier in the Eastern United States. The Ohio Hopewell culture from the Middle Woodland period 200 B.C.-A.D. 400 (Abrams 1985) produced cut mica examples of the glyph. In the Southwest, the "four directions" symbol appears on Hohokam ceramics and petroglyphs that are identified as Hohokam. This is also true of the other identified cultural groups in the prehistoric Southwest see figure 50 and photo 52.

The Zuni of New Mexico as reported by F. H. Cushing in 1896 partition space into seven regions, beginning with the four directions—north, south, east, west, then zenith, nadir and center. Each of these regions is assigned a color significance, and all things are classified according to one of these spatial indicators. The four directions are the primary directional subdivisions.

From Raven Site Ruin at the northern base of the White Mountains, three examples have been excavated to date. The exterior of a Cedar Creek Polychrome bowl is shown in photo 52 and the example consists of four "cloud" icons, i.e. unilateral terraced units, which are combined to create the glyph. According to modern residents of the site, Wendel and Ruth Sherwood, in the past, amongst the surface ceramic material, the "four directions" glyph could be found on ladle handles and large sherds. Today, however, this material has been carried away by surface collectors.

The "four directions" glyph can also be found on Athapaskan weaving. Before its association with Nazi Germany from 1939 and until the termination of the second world war, it was a common symbol on Navajo rugs (see figure 51 and 52). The swastika patterns were discouraged by the Indian traders during this period for obvious reasons; they didn't sell. It can still be seen today in Navajo weaving if one has a sharp eye. It has retained its form in the "flaming twirling log", a sand painting narrative that tells the story of the holy twins surviving the great flood on a log raft (see photo 53 and figure 53).

The "four directions" glyph is well represented and its meaning is seldom debated even by the most skeptical of scholars. The White Mountain example shown in photo 52 combines the "cloud" icon with the "four directions" symbol. The two are quite compatible. Clouds are often included in translations and representations indicating "far away" or "distant" (see translation of vessel Pi2).

Figure 50. Gilastyle petroglyph from the South Mountains, Arizona, showing the "four directions" glyph . (From Schaafsma 1980).

Photo 51. Quapaw pottery jar dating from A.D. 1650-1750 with the "four directions" glyph. (WMAC Collections)

Photo 52. Cedar Creek Polychrome sherd dating A.D. 1300-1375 (Carlson 1970) from Raven Site Ruin, Springerville, Arizona showing the "four directions" glyph composed of "cloud" icons. (WMAC Collections)

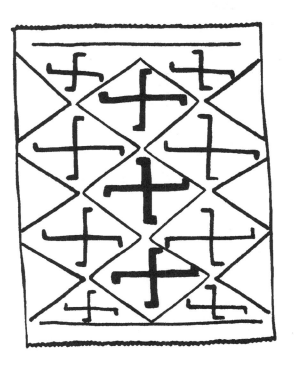

Figure 51. Navajo rug showing a variation of the "four directions" glyph. Made in the Zuni area around 1907. (From Rodee 1987)

Figure 52. Navajo rug with five swastika designs dating 1900-1920. (From Rodee 1987)

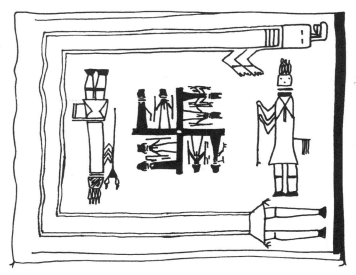

Figure 53. The "flaming, twirling log" narrative with the "four directions" icon. (From Rodee 1987)

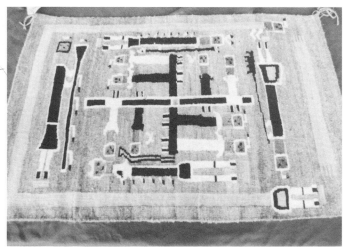

Photo 53. Navajo rug with the "flaming twirling log" creation narrative. The "four directions" glyph is still present.

HOUSE/MARRIAGE

The icon meaning "house" is deduced from the icon meaning "pueblo" (see Pueblo/Village). The "pueblo" icon consists of several interlocked unilateral terraced units, usually four pair, set in a square or rectangle, surrounded by the "earth/land" icon and bordered in a triangle representing "hill". If four paired and interlocked unilateral terraced units are a component of the "pueblo" icon, i. e. "more than one (house)" then logically one pair of interlocked unilateral terrace units, set in a square or rectangle, could represent the "house" icon. The interlocking of the two unilateral terraced units creates the square "geographical place" icon serendipitously. This icon is frequently represented on prehistoric pottery. The idea that the icon for "house" could be synonymous with "marriage" is derived by equating the single family unit with the single dwelling unit and the idea is further reenforced by the sign language gesture for "marriage" (see figure 55). The extended family is a somewhat larger concept and would include clan symbols and identities usually inherent to a larger group than simply man and woman (see "Clan Symbols"). The two interlocked terrace units set in a square, represent the man and woman interlocked, i.e. joined, in marriage, and the square or rectangular framing is equated to the four walls of the single family dwelling. The square or rectangle being equivalent to "house, lodge, dwelling" is protohistorically recognized in North America by the Hopi, Ojibwa, and Dakota (Martineau 1987:138) and the symbol is also used in Egyptian hieroglyphs for "house" (Mallery 1888-89).

The square and rectangular framing created by interlocking these terrace pairs definitely suggests property, location, house, i.e. an earthbound physical human created space. Nature does not make squares and rectangles, humankind does. It is possible that the terraced unit is one of the basic elements used by prehistoric potters to illustrate several different symbols depending upon its combination with other elements. The unit, in its singular form, is used to represent clouds, the wings of thunderbirds and many other glyphs. The single terraced unit may have a meaning unto itself, although this meaning may remain largely unknown. One example, vessel SW1012, has been found where singular unilateral terraced units are used to represent the many houses in a pueblo glyph (see "Variations of the Pueblo Glyph" in the foreword).

One of the "pueblo" icons encountered suggests a different icon for "house". Photo 54 shows a "pueblo" icon without the interlocked pairs of terraced units at center, but instead with three dots at center. This "pueblo" icon is quite small and there would not have been space enough to illustrate the interlocked pairs of terraced units at center. It would follow logically that if a "pueblo" icon has three dots at center, that is, more than one of something, then a single square with one dot at center would represent "house". These squares with single dots at center are rampant on prehistoric pottery and they may be yet another representation of the "house" icon. Prehistoric pueblos utilized single roof entrances facilitated by ladders. This roof entrance also served as a smoke hole to allow the smoke from the central hearth to escape. If you view a pueblo from a higher elevation, the square created by the four walls and the darker opening created by the central roof entrance hole very much resemble the square with a single dot at center glyph in question. This square with a dot at center for "house" is also seen on the pictographs of the Hidatsa tribe, with the dots at center representing the upright poles to support the roof (Mallery 1888-89:720). Similar designs are also found on Mayan glyphs and Egyptian hieroglyphs (see figure 54).

Examples of the "house/marriage" icon represented by the interlocked pairs of terrace units enclosed in a square include SW1003 see (photo 55), SW 1509 (see photo 56), SW715 (see photo 57) a Pinedale example, A.D. 1300-1400 (Carlson 1970:94), and finally C1-1 (see photo 58) a Reserve Black-on-white (Brody 1977:102) with the icon at center.

Examples of the "house" icon represented by the square unit with a single dot at center include: SW1509 (see photo 59); QrPi21 (see photo 60), and SW715 (see photo 61).

The present day Hopi translate a common petroglyph as "migration." This glyph often consists of two interlocked terraced units, i.e. "house/marriage" with a spiralling line which connects another similar interlocked terraced glyph. Equating the idea of "house/marriage" to the extended family or clan, it is easy to recognize that a migration of a clan or "house" to another location as represented by this petroglyph (see photo 62).

The American sign language gesture for "marriage" is shown in figure 55. It consists of the palms of the hands clasped together, just as the terraced units are interlocked. The gesture for house is also given in figure 56 (Costello 1985:40,17). It consists of a representation of a single house roof and walls. The gesture demonstrates the peaked roof of modern dwellings, as would be expected. Prehistorically the gesture should reproduce the form of the habitation units of the period. Figure 57 demonstrates the sign language of the Hidatsa, Kiowa, Arikara, Comanche, Apache, and the Wichita (Mallery 1879-80:428) showing the fingers locked together gesturally demonstrating the interlocked logs used in the house construction of the period.

Figure 54. Pictograph, petroglyph and hieroglyph showing "house", Hidatsa, Mayan, and Egyptian respectively. (From Mallery 1888-89:720, 722)

Photo 54. Tularosa sherd, A.D. 1200-1300 (Carlson 1970) showing "pueblo" icon with three dots at center. Excavated from the Raven Site Ruin, Springerville, Arizona. (WMAC Collections)

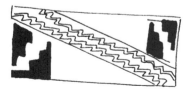

Photo 55. SW1003 Tularosa vessel, dating A.D.1200-1300 (Carlson1970) showing two "house/marriage" icons created from the icon for "flight" extending from the unilateral "cloud" symbol to the right. This "house/cloud" combination represents the second of the twelve prehistoric Hopi phratries, Patki, or "house/cloud" or "water/house". The lightning symbol between the "house/cloud" glyph is the icon of a dependent clan, the Talawipiki. (Hodge 1907-10). (WMAC Collections)

Photo 56. SW1509 Unnamed Red-on-buff A.D. 1450 (Woodbury and Woodbury 1966) "house/marriage" icon with "cloud" attributes. The square and rectangular framing of these terrace pairs definitely suggests property, location, i.e. house. (WMAC Collections)

Photo 57. SW715 Pinedale Black-on-white olla, dating A.D. 1275-1325 (Carlson 1970:53) with "house/marriage" icon. Excavated at the Raven Site Ruin, Springerville, Arizona. (WMAC Collections)

Photo 58. C1-1 Reserve Black-on-white bowl with "house/marriage" icon at center. (WMAC Collections)

 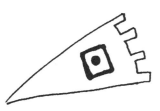

Photo 59. SW1509 Unnamed Red-on-buff vessel dating around A.D. 1450 (Woodbury and Woodbury 1966) showing "house/marriage" icon represented by squares with dots at center. This "house/marriage icon is superimposed upon the icon for "cloud" which creates the prehistoric Hopi clan symbol Patki or "cloud/house". See vessel translation SW1509. (WMAC Collections)

Photo 60. QrPi21 Tonto Polychrome olla, showing "house/marriage" icon as squares with dots at center. (WMAC Collections)

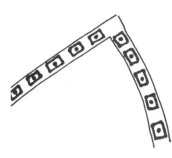

Photo 61. Pinedale Black-on-white olla dating A.D. 1275-1325 (Carlson 1970) showing "house/marriage" icon as squares with dots in center.

Photo 62. Petroglyph translated as "migration" by the present day Hopi. The "house" or clan migrated (connecting line) to another location. Raven Site Ruin, Springerville, Arizona.

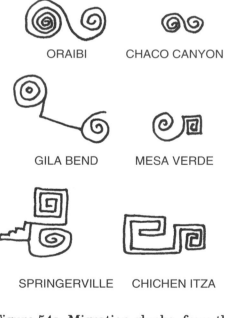

ORAIBI   CHACO CANYON

GILA BEND   MESA VERDE

SPRINGERVILLE   CHICHEN ITZA

Figure 54a. Migration glyphs from the Southwest. (From Walters 1977)

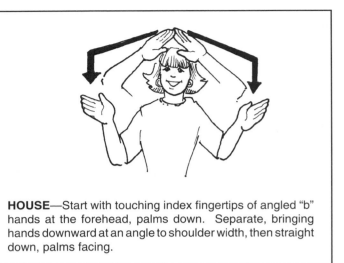

HOUSE—Start with touching index fingertips of angled "b" hands at the forehead, palms down. Separate, bringing hands downward at an angle to shoulder width, then straight down, palms facing.

Fig. 56. American sign language gesture for "house". Gesture demonstrates the outline of a modern house with peaked roof. (From Costello 1983)

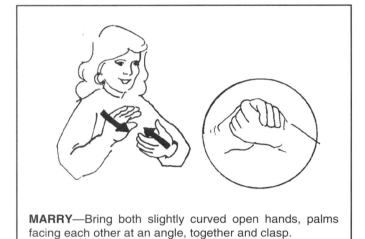

MARRY—Bring both slightly curved open hands, palms facing each other at an angle, together and clasp.

Figure 55. American sign language gesture for "marriage", the clasped hands resembling the interlocked terraced units found on the pottery icon (From Costello 1983)

Figure 57. The North American Indian sign language gesture for "house/lodge" with the interlocked fingers representing stacked logs (From Mallery 1879-80:428)

LIGHTNING

It is not surprising that an icon for lightning can be found on prehistoric Southwest pottery. Weather elements associated with rain are very common due to the marginal environment.

An excellent and undeniable example of the "lightning" ideograph can be found on vessel Qr15 (see photo 63). This Salado Polychrome bowl shows two lightning icons at center with the "earth/land" icon, and the "wind/falling rain" symbols on the inside rim of the bowl. Although this vessel was excavated below the Mogollon Rim, the Salado Polychromes are believed to have been influenced by the White Mountain Redwares (Steen 1966). The overall translation of the bowl is "storm". There may be more significance in the design of this bowl than just a pictorial representation of a thunderstorm. According to Zuni legend, the eight gods of the storms changed the twin children of the sun into guardian warriors more powerful than monsters, gods or men (Cushing 1901). In Hopi legend, the idea of "storm" has been personified into a single deity named Hukangwaa who assisted the warrior twins after a smoking test (Mullet 1979).

The Hopi Indian "rain" symbol illustrated in figure 58 shows the "lightning" icon radiating out from the clouds (Cushing 1882-83). This more recent representation includes an "arrow point" icon on the end of the lightning. Similar "lightning" representations found on petroglyphs near Oakley Springs, Arizona, are shown in figure 59 (Mallery 1882-83). This "arrow point" can also be found on "lightning" symbols on the prehistoric pottery from Sikyatki (see figure 60) (Fewkes 1895). With this lightning symbol, not only is the "arrow point" present, but the lightning is emanating from the mouth of a serpent. Serpents are often associated with the lightning symbol, and in the iconography it is sometimes difficult to distinguish between the two, especially when the icons are found in a very reduced form as is often the case with petroglyphs, probably due to the difficult nature of the pecked stone media. Also found in figure 60 are the two intersecting lines behind the "arrow point". These two lines cause a remarkable similarity of the Sikyatki icon to representations of headdresses on Mimbres vessels. These Mimbres headdresses are assumed to be fish skeletons, and other Mimbres vessels do indeed clearly demonstrate fish skel-

etons in isolation (Brody 1977, Cosgrove and Cosgrove 1932, Moulard 1984, et al.) (see figures 61 and 62). The obvious difference between the Sikyatki representation and the Hopi representation, when compared to the Mimbres headdresses, is the absence of the all essential zigzag motion line as the basic "lightning" element. As is often the case with the Classic Black-on-white vessels, the Mimbres representation is realistic. It depicts an actual headdress and these representations are not icons.

There is probably an association between the lightning and snake representations that goes beyond their similarity in form. The two are often found interrelated as in figure 60. Figure 63, from Jemez Pueblo 1888-89 as recorded by W.H. Jackson shows the "lightning" icon with a serpent head, and figure 64 illustrates a Pinedale Polychrome bowl from the White Mountains dating A.D. 1275-1325 (Carlson 1970). This Pinedale bowl representation combines elements of both serpent and lightning, including the "arrow point" icon head, the zigzag lightning body, and "water/rain" dots along the corpus of the symbol. Photo 64 again shows the serpent with the zigzag lightning body, this time decorating a Fremont effigy vessel from Utah.

One of the problems inherent with the icon for "lightning" is the symbol's similarity in form to other icons such as "river", "confusion/fear", and obviously "serpent". Even in the presence of other weather elements it is often inconclusive to interpret. The icon for "lightning" probably holds other nuances of meaning such as virility, strength or destruction, which are not necessarily limited to its association with the coming of rain. Lightning is also thought to represent a pathway, much like the symbolic use of rainbows and the Milky Way.

The zigzag form of the lightning icon also appears in the negative between the interlocked terraced units representing "house/marriage", "clouds" and other iconographic representations. Evidence that these combinations represent various prehistoric Hopi clan symbols is presented in the translation of vessel SW1509.

A representation of the "cloud" icon and its association with lightning is shown in figure 65, the Hopi Indian's representation of the god "Umtakina" or "the thunder" (Mallery 1888-89.) This representation illustrates the negative "lightning" icon in between two unilateral terraced "cloud" units complete with the semi-circular "cloud" units repeated laterally as a redundant element. However, the negative "lightning" icon often appears between the unilateral terraced units simply because of the shape of the units. Perhaps the semi-circular domed units seen in figure 65 were necessary to clarify that the unilateral units were indeed "clouds" and that the negative zigzag is indeed "lightning".

In Athapaskan sandpainting ceremonies, one chant is used to cure the effects of lightning, arrows and snakes. The relationship here is most likely based on the similarity of the motion of all three. It is interesting to notice in these sandpainting creations, when lightning is represented as female it is made with a zigzag line with an intersecting line near the end. When it is created as a male lightning form, the zigzag line is the same, but at the end there is an arrow point. These two depictions look remarkably similar to our modern male and female symbolic representations (see figure 66).

Another example where the negative "lightning" icon appears between the unilateral terraced units, and where the meaning is probably not "lightning" but instead "confusion/fear" in accord with Athapaskan symbolism, is vessel SW1011. This Fourmile Polychrome dating A.D. 1325-1400 (Carlson 1970) is not a weather element combination, but rather a "pueblo" icon complete with the "earth/land" icon around the village, and surrounded by "arrow point" icons. The central glyph in vessel SW1011 probably represents "confusion/fear" as compared to the sign language gesture. The vessel's overall translation is "siege" (see photo 65).

Vessel SW1003 is a Tularosa Black-on-white olla dating A.D. 1200-1300 (see photo 66). The zigzag representation in this case separates two opposing "house" icons created by the interlocking of the "flight" icons extending from a unilateral "cloud" glyph. These symbols appear above a "night sky" checkerboard. There is a positive "lightning"

mirrored by two negative icons, or is the positive "lightning" icon the accidental result of producing the two negatives? Again the difficulties with the form of the "lightning" icon is illustrated. Vessel SW1003 most likely presents symbols in combination that are the prehistoric Hopi clan representation for Patki "cloud/house" and Talawipiki "lightning" which is a dependent clan of the Patki phratral group.

The "lightning" icon is usually composed of a positive zigzag body, sometimes accompanied by the "arrow point" icon on one end, and often associated with serpents or weather elements. The icon for "confusion/fear", although also a zigzag form, has so far only been observed in the negative and is only speculatively identified within the context of a larger translation and Navajo mythology.

The sign language used among the North American Indians during the nineteenth century included a gesture for lightning. According to Mallery:

"The part relating specially to the streak is portrayed in an Indian gesture sign as follows: Right hand elevated before and above the head, forefinger pointing upward, brought down with great rapidity with a sinuous, undulating motion, finger still extended diagonally downward toward the right."

The modern American sign language gesture for "lightning" is illustrated below. It is nearly identical to the prehistoric glyph and to the proto-historic gesture described by Mallery. Other gestures illustrated are "fear", "river", and "serpent". All share similar attributes. The inherent motion of rivers, serpents, lightning and possibly even the flight path of arrows cause ambiguity of this icon if found in isolation. The frequent occurrence of zigzag icons is probably due to not only the importance of lightning as a common weather element, but also because the glyph represents a wide range of ideas based primarily on the motion or movement inherent to the ideas represented, its destructive potential, and the pathway created by its appearance in the sky.

Modern American sign language gestures for "lightning", the gestures mimic motion. (From Butterworth and Flodin 1983) (Costello 1983)

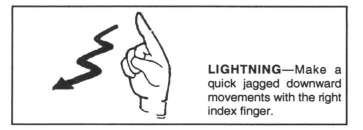

LIGHTNING—Make a quick jagged downward movements with the right index finger.

SNAKE—Move the right index finger forward in small spiral circles as it passes under the downturned palm of the left flat hand. *Alternative* (not illustrated: Move the right V fingers forward with circular or winding movements.

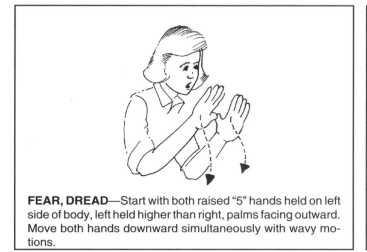

FEAR, DREAD—Start with both raised "5" hands held on left side of body, left held higher than right, palms facing outward. Move both hands downward simultaneously with wavy motions.

RIVER—Tap the index finger side of the right "w" hand, palm left, to the chin. Bring both downturned open hands, left hand closer to body than right, forward while wiggling the fingers.

Modern American sign language for " serpent, fear and river"; the gestures mimic motion. (From Butterworth and Flodin 1983) (Costello 1983)

Photo 63, Qr15, Salado Polychrome bowl. Lightning appears at center between two "earth/land" icons. Around the inside rim are the icons for "wind" and "falling rain". (WMAC Collections)

Figure 58. Hopi "rain" symbol showing the "lightning" ideogram complete with an "arrow point" icon attached. (From Cushing 1882-83)

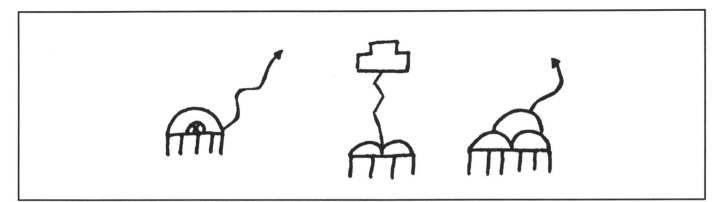

Figure 59. Petroglyphs from Oakley Springs, Arizona, showing three forms of "lightning" representations. The "cloud" and "rain" glyphs help identify the "lightning" icon, which otherwise could be mistaken for "river", "snake" or other similar iconographic forms. (From Mallery 1882-83)

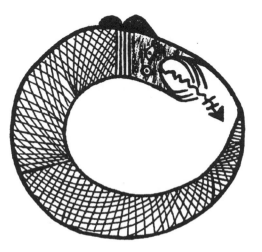

Figure 60. Sikyatki "lightning" icon emanating from the mouth of a serpent. The zigzag representation includes an "arrow point" attached and two intersecting lines of unknown meaning. These intersecting lines give the icon a similar appearance to Mimbres headdresses, although the two are probably not related. (From Fewkes 1895)

Figure 61. Classic Mimbres Black-on-white bowl showing the fish bone headdresses. The similarity to the Sikyatki symbol is evident, but the headdresses lack the basic zigzag element necessary for the "lightning" icon. The headdresses are realistic representations, not icons. (From Moulard 1984)

Figure 62. Classic Mimbres Black-on-white bowl showing fish skeleton in isolation. This is a fairly common theme on Mimbres bowls and it may have had a special meaning to the Mimbres people. (From Moulard 1984)

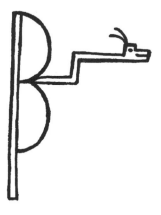

Figure 63. Painting from Jemez Pueblo, New Mexico recorded by W.H. Jackson in 1888 showing the "lightning" symbol with a plumed serpent's head. Serpents and the "lightning" icon are commonly combined. (From Mallery 1888-89)

Figure 64. Pinedale Polychrome bowl with serpent. The zigzag body form complete with "arrow point" head and "water/rain" icons along the body show a strong association with the "lightning" symbolism. A White Mountain Redware dating A.D. 1275-1325. (From Carlson 1970)

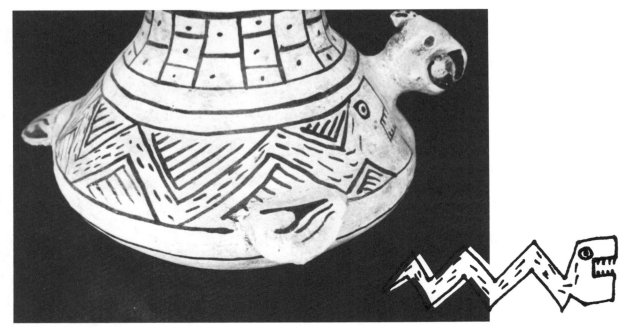

Photo 64. Fremont effigy vessel with serpent. This representation again shows the zigzag body similar to the lightning form. (WMAC Collections)

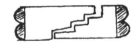

Figure 65. Hopi symbol representing Umtak-ina "the thunder" showing the "lightning" glyph as the negative, resulting from the interlocking of the unilateral terraced units meaning "clouds". (From Mallery 1888-89)

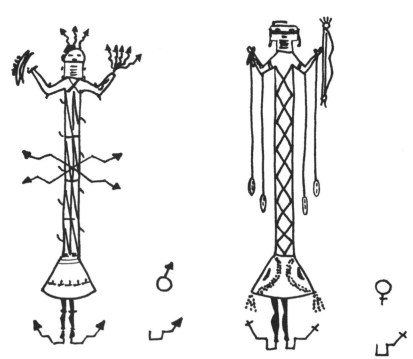

Figure 66. Navajo sandpainting designs showing "lightning" with male and female attributes radiating from the feet of the figures. The sex of each figure is identified accordingly. The similarity to our modern male and female symbols is remarkable. (From Newcomb and Reichard 1975)

Photo 65. SW1011 Fourmile Polychrome bowl showing a "pueblo" icon surrounded by "earth/land" and again surrounded by attacking "arrow point" icons. The vessel translation is "siege" and the pronounced zigzag icon at center could possibly represent "confusion/fear". (WMAC Collections)

Photo 66. Tularosa Black-on-white olla, SW1003, showing two opposing houses over a "night sky" with "lightning" icons between the "houses". This olla probably represents the prehistoric Hopi clans Patki "cloud/house" and Talawipiki "lightning". (WMAC Collections)

LIZARD/MAN

There has been some confusion between male anthromorphic figures and figures that represent lizards. In the reduced forms presented on petroglyphs and pictographs the two are difficult to differentiate. Examples of what appear to be well-endowed male figures abound in the rock art of the Southwest (see figure 67). The question has been raised as to whether or not these might instead be representations of lizards, the tail of the lizard being mistaken for the phallus. These figures have also been encountered on the pottery of the White Mountains, and an excellent example is shown in photo 67. Other ceramic examples from other areas also use the symbol (see figure 68).

At Salmon Ruins near Bloomfield, New Mexico, a recent excavation from a kiva on a PIII site has revealed a "lizard-woman" effigy. In light of this discovery the anthromorphic lizard may have been an intentional distortion, and may be a combined form having supernatural significance (Schaafsma 80).

There is one element to the figure which should be considered when trying to distinguish between the lizard form and simply the male human form, leaving the possibility of a combined figure for the moment. The abdominal area if represented solely by a line may indicate a male human, accepting the fact that both forms in question always have the tail/penis present. If the abdominal area is enlarged, fattened, then the representation greatly resembles the several Iguanidae of the Southwest.

There are many species of lizards in the Southwest that bear a striking resemblance to this icon. Obviously the horned toad which is common throughout the Southwest and often distinctly featured on Hohokam ceramics is one (see figure 69). The horned toad displays the large flattened stomach common to several of the desert Iguanidae and similar to many of the glyphs. Many of these lizards also use a behavioral mechanism for courtship and conflict where they prominently display the abdomen with its bright colors, and several species are readily capable of standing erect on their hind feet (Schmidt and Inger 1975). An even greater similarity is observed between the glyphs and the lizards when the animal has lost its tail while escaping a predator. Iguanidae have the ability of detaching their tail deliberately when it is grasped. After the attack the tail-stub completes the image created in the rock art. Figure 70 shows the "fatter" lizard form with a stub-tail.

The phallic symbol is common on both ceramics and rock art in the Southwest. It is very commonly found on the Kokopelli figure with his humped back and flute (see figure 71). This figure first appears during BIII times and continues throughout prehistory (Schaafsma 1980). The phallus is also commonly displayed on Mimbres ceramics both as inanimate staffs and extremely animated depictions of copulation (see figures 72 and 73) (Moulard 84). The question whether or not these glyphs are men or lizards really depends upon whether the representation between the legs is a penis or a tail, or both if the figure is representing some combined form.

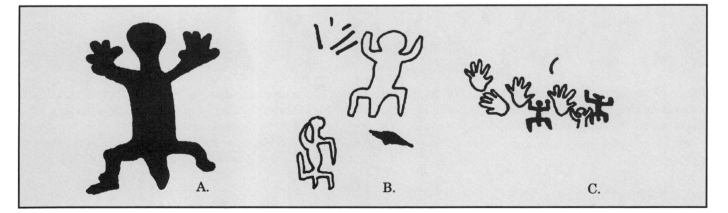

Figure 67, A (From Barnes 1982) B and C (From Schaafsma 1980) showing the disputed "lizard/man" glyph.

Photo 67. SW1008 St. Johns Polychrome bowl (underfired) dating A.D. 1175-1300 showing the "lizard/man" figure. (WMAC Collections)

Figure 67a. Tusayan bowl with "lizard/man" icon. (From Holmes 1882)

Figure 68. Reserve Black-on-white effigy canteen, circa. A.D. 950-1150 with two "lizard/men" icons. (From Moulard 1984)

Figure 69. Horned toad effigy on Hohokam ceramics. (From Haury 1978)

Figure 70. "Lizard/man" glyph from the South Mountains, Arizona, showing the fatter "lizard/man" form. (From Schaafsma 1980)

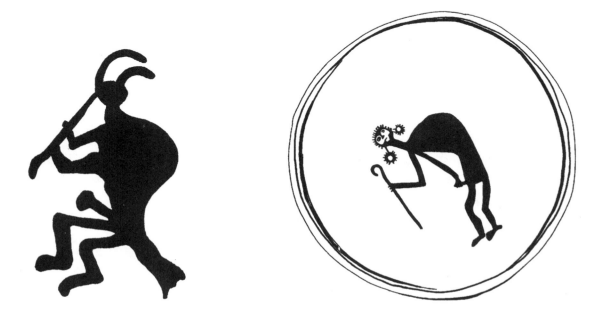

Figure 71. (a) Kokopelli glyph from the La Cieneguilla area (From Barnes 1982) and (b) a Mimbres Black-on-white bowl. (From Brody 1977)

Figure 72. Mimbres vessel showing ritual scene of copulation with eight figures. (From Moulard 1984)

Figure 73. Mimbres Black-on-white bowl A.D. 950-1150. Copulation scene with phallic staff. (From Moulard 1984)

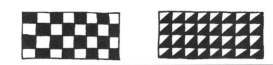

NIGHT SKY/DAY SKY

The night sky and the day sky are represented primarily by the "things found in the sky", that is, an area of the vessel will be painted with representations of the sun, moon, rainbows, clouds, birds, stars, and possibly even stars exploding (see appendix I). The "sky" is simply the area or surface of the vessel, the area around the object depicted. In this section, the representations of things found in the sky as depicted in the culture of the Southwest will be demonstrated.

During his stay with the Zuni in the nineteenth century, F. H. Cushing observed that in Zuni mythology, the sky is represented by the inverted terrace, mimicking the terraced appearance of the horizon where the sky meets the mesa. It is not difficult to demonstrate this inverted terrace on pottery both prehistoric and historic.

Also recorded in Zuni lore is the story of the creation of the planet Mars and the Milky Way.

The warrior twins Matsailema and Ahaiyuta killed and beheaded the monster Atahsaia. Ahaiyuta threw the head into the sky and it became Mokwanosana the "lying star", which rises in the summer and tells of the coming morning when it is only midnight. Then the brother Matsailema disemboweled the monster and flung the entrails into the sky, creating the Milky Way. The warrior twins themselves are represented in the night sky by the morning and evening stars which follow just before and just after their father the sun. (Cushing 1979)

The most commonly recognized symbol for the "night sky" is a checkerboard pattern, often illustrated as a band, or even a zigzag band. This checkerboard is thought to represent the Milky Way, and is widely accepted in academe as the icon for "night sky". In Pueblo symbolism, the night sky and the Milky Way are the home of the war gods, and the pathway used by the warrior spirits (Moulard 1984). The Zuni clown society, the Ne'wekwe, dominate over the night sky, the winter, and the underworld. When the Ne'wekwe clowns appear in public, they are striped from head to foot with lateral black and white bands (Wright 1985).

Their body paint is symbolic of the Milky Way which is said to be used by them as a means of travel in the same way that it is used by their patron deity, Payatamuy. In Zuni lore, the colors black and white, are also associated with the directions nadir and zenith. The idea that the checkerboard pattern represents a pathway for deities across the night sky is well exemplified by the nature of its use on prehistoric pottery. The checkerboard often appears as a band or even as a zigzag pathway (see figures 74 and 75). Interestingly, this pattern is often found decorating the backs of serpents. Serpents also often appear in a zigzag depiction, symbolizing lightning, rain, ground waters, and movement. They are an earth, sky, and water creature in Pre-Columbian Meso-American and contemporary Southwest religion and they are associated with the fertility of corn through their water bringing (or withholding) abilities. Figure 76, a Casas Grandes Ramos Polychrome jar dating A.D. 1200-1340, depicts a very interesting combination of serpent, checkerboard, and zigzag pattern. The zigzag pattern is achieved by alternating the grid of the checkerboard within the area of the serpent's back. Figure 77 again shows a serpent, this time in the form of an effigy canteen, with both the checkerboard "night sky" glyph and "lightning" icons in association. This combination deserves further attention. The combination of the serpent, lightning and the checkerboard/Milky Way could be due to a combined glyph meaning or, more likely, because all three can illustrate a pathway or road. Serpents are combined in many ways with many other icons, and they hold an important place in prehistoric iconography. The religious aspects of the serpent first entered the Southwest from Mexico with the Hohokam. In Mexican iconography, the serpent is represented with bird and water symbols. In this way, the serpent may be a representation of the earth, the bird the sky, and the rain/water the medium between the two.

The checkerboard "night sky" symbol is common in the White Mountain iconography, and many examples exist. Vessel SW1003 (see photo 68), illustrates the "night sky" checkerboard below a combination of glyphs thought to represent "two houses in conflict". SW300, a Tularosa Black-on-

White olla demonstrates the checkerboard "night sky" (see photo 69).

A variation of the checkerboard pattern is a grid with a dot at center. This glyph is thought to represent "corn" (see "Corn").

The checkerboard pattern is best described as a representation of the Milky Way, a pathway for deities. This is not really a "night sky" glyph as much as it is an actual thing found in the night sky. This being the case with the search for a generic "sky" glyph, we see things in the sky illustrated, but no one glyph that solely translates "sky", with the possible exception of the inverted terrace recorded by Cushing.

Other than the checkerboard icon, one other depiction of the Milky Way can be found in the symbolism of the Navajo. Even though the Athapaskan speakers arrived somewhat late in the Southwest, the majority of their mythology seems to be directly related to the Pueblo peoples who inhabited the area for millennia. Found in their sandpaintings, which are used in curing ceremonies and which reflect the ancient lore of the Navajo, there is a representation of the Milky Way which consists of a zigzag diamond pattern (see figure 78). Also discovered among the sandpainting symbolic repertoire of the Navajo are other "night sky" objects. Big stars are represented by a cross, and specific constellations are also frequently represented (Newcomb and Reichard 1975). The use of the cross to represent stars has also been observed in petroglyphs and pictographs. The "star ceiling" of the rock alcoves of Canyon de Chelly may have been produced during the Navajo occupation of the canyon. The use of the cross to represent the larger stars and possibly even the planets can often be found on the prehistoric pottery of the Southwest although definitive translation is difficult.

Recent studies which re-examine Classic Mimbres Black-on-white bowls have concluded that many of these vessels illustrate the night sky. The primary depiction which is the key to these investigations is the rabbit. The rabbit in Mimbrenos' thought is the representative of the moon. Many other cultures worldwide recognize the form of the rabbit on the surface of the moon, dissimilar to our Western "man in the moon". Prehistorically, the Chinese and the Mayan cultures also depicted a rabbit when referring to lunar phenomena (Schele 1977). When Mimbres bowls with rabbit represen-

tations were examined, and numerical analysis was applied to other features found on these bowls, in all cases the numbers discovered were lunar numbers (Robbins 1991). In Meso-American depictions the rabbit is associated with fertility, sexuality, frolicking and drunkenness. In Mayan depictions, the rabbit is the scribe in charge of hieroglyphics. Also found on Classic Mimbres Black-on-white pottery are depictions of rabbits being eaten by birds. It is a common Amerindian theme that an eclipse is represented by something eating the sun or the moon (Heizer 1974). These rabbit and bird combinations could represent lunar or solar eclipse (see appendix I).

The American sign language gesture for "night" is shown in figure 79. It is a depiction of the sun going below the horizon. It is not surprising that there is no similarity between the gesture and the checkerboard glyph. The gesture represents the idea of "night", and the checkerboard glyph represents the Milky Way. However, if we accept that the checkerboard pattern is the Milky Way, a star cluster, then the American sign language gesture for "star, starred" is an acceptable match (see figure 80).

Day Sky

Because of what we have learned with the "night sky" analysis, it may appear futile to seek a "day sky" glyph. We should expect to discover many things that appear in the day sky—rainbows, the sun, etc. but a singular representation of "day sky" may elude research. As with the "night sky" treatment, there is most likely not a true "day sky" icon, as much as there are representations of things found in the day sky. The best example is the rainbow. The rainbow definitely depicts a daytime representation as would an icon for the "sun". Like the Milky Way, rainbows are used as pathways by supernaturals in Pueblo mythology (Moulard 1984). Rainbows are also associated with the earliest representations of the "flute player" or Kokopelli in the rock imagery of the Southwest. This depiction dates as early as BIII in the Chinle style (Schaafsma 1980). The American sign language gesture for "rainbow" is illustrated in figure 81. It is not surprising that the gestural representation is nearly identical to the prehistoric glyph.

One geometric design discovered in White Mountain iconography which may represent a more generic "day sky" glyph is found on vessel SW1003 (see photo 70). This vessel seems to represent opposites, war and peace, harmony and conflict, and possibly day and night (see vessel translation SW1003). The "night sky", i.e. the Milky Way checkerboard, is represented in one set of panels. The opposing set, and possibly the opposite set of meanings, illustrates a glyph made up of a grid with each square diagonally bisected and one half negative and one positive. This icon could be a "day sky" or "daylight" representation. These diagonally bisected, black and white squares create a grid similar in nature to the "Milky Way" checkerboard. This icon does resemble refracted sunlight. When the glyph on vessel SW1003 was compared to the American sign language gesture for "day", the similarity is surprising (see figure 82). Hopefully, with future excavations, more vessels that utilize this glyph will see the light of the "day sky".

Figure 74. Classic Mimbres Black-on-white bowl dating A.D. 950-1150 showing the zigzag checkerboard pattern. This depiction illustrates the idea of the Milky Way as a pathway for deities. (From Moulard 1984)

Figure 75. Classic Mimbres Black-on-white bowl A.D. l950-1150 showing the checkerboard zigzag. (From Moulard 1984)

Figure 76. Casas Grandes Ramos Polychrome jar A.D. 1205-1340 showing a serpent with zigzag checkerboard. The zigzag pathway effect is created by altering the positive and negative squares within the grid. (From Moulard 1984)

Figure 77. Tularosa Black-on-white effigy canteen A.D. 1100-1250 showing the checkerboard pattern in association with the serpent form and the symbol for lightning (From Moulard 1984)

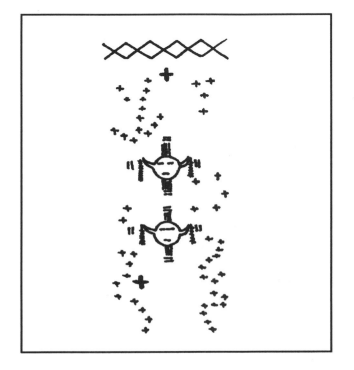

Figure 78. Navajo sandpainting representations of the "night sky". The linked diamonds symbolize the Milky Way and the larger stars are shown as crosses. Specific constellations are depicted depending upon when the sandpainting is made and which constellations are visible at that time. (From Reichard 1977)

Photo 68. SW1003. Tularosa Black-on-white olla with checkerboard "night sky" glyph. The opposite panel of this vessel shows a possible icon for "day sky" or "daylight". (WMAC Collections)

Photo 69. SW300. Tularosa Black-on-white olla with checkerboard "night sky" pattern. (WMAC Collections)

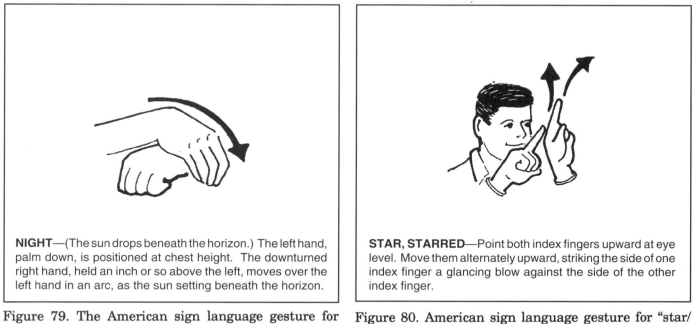

Photo 70. SW1003. Tularosa Black-on-white olla A.D. 1200-1300 (From Carlson 1970) showing a very possible "day sky" glyph. The opposite panel illustrates the "night sky" checkerboard icon, and the vessel's overall translations seem to indicate contrasting ideas. (WMAC Collections)

NIGHT—(The sun drops beneath the horizon.) The left hand, palm down, is positioned at chest height. The downturned right hand, held an inch or so above the left, moves over the left hand in an arc, as the sun setting beneath the horizon.

STAR, STARRED—Point both index fingers upward at eye level. Move them alternately upward, striking the side of one index finger a glancing blow against the side of the other index finger.

Figure 79. The American sign language gesture for "night". This represents the sun going below the horizon and is not really related to the checkerboard glyph which represents the Milky Way. (From Sternberg 1987)

Figure 80. American sign language gesture for "star/starred". (From Butterworth and Flodin 1983)

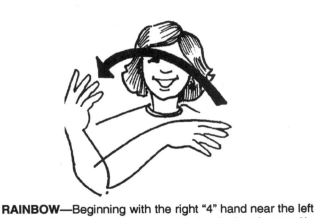

RAINBOW—Beginning with the right "4" hand near the left shoulder, fingers pointing outward, bring the hand upward in an arc, keeping the palm toward the body and ending near right shoulder.

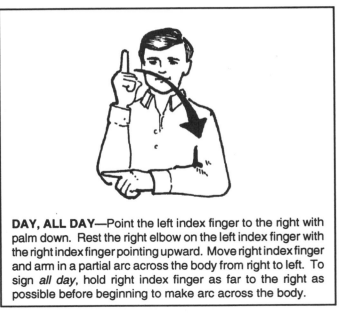

DAY, ALL DAY—Point the left index finger to the right with palm down. Rest the right elbow on the left index finger with the right index finger pointing upward. Move right index finger and arm in a partial arc across the body from right to left. To sign *all day*, hold right index finger as far to the right as possible before beginning to make arc across the body.

Figure 81. American sign language gesture for "rainbow". It is not surprising that the prehistoric glyph and the gesture are nearly identical. (Costello 1983)

Figure 82. The American sign language gesture for "day", a remarkable match to the glyph shown in photo 70, vessel SW1003. (Butterworth and Flodin 1983)

PROPERTY/OWNERSHIP/HUMAN CREATED SPACE

The prehistoric icon in the Southwest that represents "property" is a square or rectangle. Other glyphs are generally included with the symbol to detail the nature of the "property" glyph because in isolation, the symbol says very little. As so many physical things involve a geographical place the "property" icon is often represented with its "place" meaning employed. This use of the icon's "place" interpretation probably was the original representation. Gardens, houses and pueblos were pictographically illustrated with square and rectangular sides because that is how they physically appeared during the temporal period when the icons were in use. Settlement patterns in the Southwest shifted after A.D. 1150, developing larger villages utilizing square room blocks. There was an architectural shift from the round pit houses of earlier periods to the square rooms utilized almost universally by P III. This architectural style was well developed by A.D. 1200 in the White Mountain area (Cordell 1984). Photo 71 shows the icon used in the symbol for "pueblo" illustrating a geographical place and photo 72 shows the icon for "house/marriage" again incorporating the symbol. The transition from the "place" meaning, i.e. house, garden, town, to the idea of "property/ownership" is natural enough in human nature. The idea of my house, my garden, my town might seem to contradict the modern illusion that altruistic Indians didn't believe in ownership, but the facts are quite contradictory. As soon as human beings plant and tend crops, a heightened sense of land ownership comes into play (MacNeish 1986, Martineau 1987).

The square and rectangular "property" icon is used to represent ownership when incorporated with clan symbols (see "Clan Symbols"). These glyphs are possession indicators, signatures and/or family names. The presence of the combined glyph indicates "this is the property of...." (see photo 73).

A square spiral produces an interesting combination of ideas. Spirals basically indicate motion and they are usually employed to illustrate "smoke" or "wind". When combined with the square or rectangular "property" symbol, the translation becomes "moving, i.e. descending/ascending onto my property." These glyphs are commonly found as petroglyphic property markers (Kearns 1973) (see figure 83).

Another interesting combination of the "property" icon with another symbol is shown in figure 84. Throughout the Southwest, petroglyphs and pictographs depicting square and rectangular animals can be found. Most researchers dismiss these as crude depictions representing generic quadrupeds (Barnes 1982)

More recently these depictions have been given more significance. A generic profiled quadruped is thought to represent movement in a particular direction, depending upon the positioning of the glyph. The reason that quadrupeds are used instead of anthromorphs, even though the depiction may actually be about people traveling, may be because a biped is difficult to illustrate moving in one direction or another. The use of a quadruped solves this problem. This explanation also helps explain the overabundance of certain animals in rock art representations such as mountain goats (Martineau 1987). When the "property" icon is given zoomorphic features, and if the zoomorphs do indeed depict movement/travel, then the translation of the symbol would be "they traveled with property".

An example of a more realistic animal combined with a "property" icon is reported by Schoolcraft and Garrick Mallery in 1879 (Mallery 1879-80). The shoulder blade of a buffalo found on the plains of Texas (see figure 85) illustrates an encounter between an Indian on horseback and two non-Indians. The buffalo in the pictograph appears with a squared hindquarters which is the "property" icon. The buffalo is also bisected with the front half painted black and the rear half painted white. This treatment indicates that the buffalo was contested property, and the rest of the depiction indicates a conflict over possession of the buffalo.

The glyph for "property" is very universal as indicated by the chart in figure 86. North American Indians, the Sumerian, Egyptian, Chinese and the Aztec all use the square or rectangle to represent a geographical place.

The American sign language gesture for "place" is shown in figure 87. When making the gesture, either a circle or square can be created, and the similarity between the prehistoric glyph and the modern sign is evident.

Photo 71. QrPi20. Salado Polychrome bowl with "pueblo" icon which incorporates the "property" icon. (WMAC Collections)

Photo 72. Vessel C1-1. Reserve Black-on-white with "house/marriage" icon which incorporates the square outline of the "property" icon. (WMAC Collections)

Photo 73. Vessel SW1501. Point of Pines Polychrome bowl showing the "property" icon at center with zoomorphic features added. These features probably represent a clan name. (WMAC Collections)

Figure 83. A squared spiral, indicating "movement onto property" or "migration". Glen Canyon (From Schaafsma 1980)

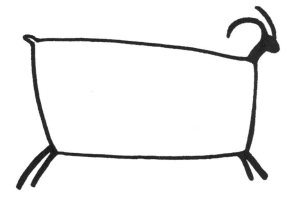

Figure 84. Square bodied quadruped. These abundant representations may indicate "movement with property" rather than being "just poorly executed". From Sevenmile Canyon, Utah. (From Barnes 1982)

Figure 85. Comanche depiction executed on the shoulder blade of a buffalo. The representation of the animal in the glyph transmits the idea of "contested property". (From Mallery 1879-80)

North American Indian	Sumerian	Egyptian	Chinese	Aztec
☐ Area or Object	☐ Garden	☐ House	▯ Enclosure	☐ Place

Figure 86. The chart shows the worldwide use of the "property/place" icon. (From Martineau 1987)

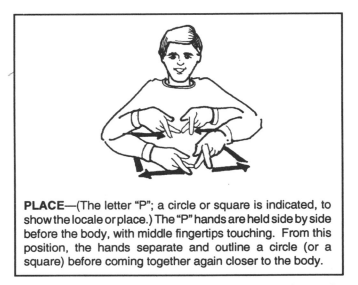

PLACE—(The letter "P"; a circle or square is indicated, to show the locale or place.) The "P" hands are held side by side before the body, with middle fingertips touching. From this position, the hands separate and outline a circle (or a square) before coming together again closer to the body.

Figure 87. The American sign language gesture for "place". The gesture can be made indicating a circle or a square. (From Butterworth and Flodin 1983)

PUEBLO/VILLAGE

Also see "The Smoking Gun". The "pueblo" icon consists of several interlocked terraced units, usually four, creating a square or rectangular larger unit, surrounded by the "earth/land" icon. Very often the icon is completed by a triangular boundary representing a hill or mountain.

Evidence that square or rectangular symbols represent a geographical place or property is virtually worldwide (see figure 86 in "property, ownership, geographical place") and is also prevalent throughout proto-historic North American Indian groups. The use of interlocked terraces to represent terraced stone buildings is also well documented, and the correlation is not difficult to visualize (see figure 88). The symbol often appears on petroglyphs and pictographs throughout the Southwest and is frequently figured with other relevant icono-graphic representations including the "earth/land" icon and "migration" (see photo 74 and figure 89)

The icon representing "pueblo" is frequent on pottery from A.D. 1200 through the early Zuni glazes of the late 1400's although in these later representations the meaning may be lost.

Anasazi settlement patterns after A.D. 1150 were characterized by trends toward increasing population aggregation and the development of larger villages (Hill 1970:88; Dean 1970:151; Zubrow 1972:137). The icon for "pueblo/village" can be seen on several Tularosa style vessels A.D. 1200-1300 (Carlson 1970:91) and later on vessels of the Fourmile style up until A.D. 1400. After this period in the White Mountains, the vitreous pre-Zuni glazes appear. The "pueblo" icon is still present, but is not seen used in context with other icons with relevant meaning. This could indicate that its meaning had declined into the "plaid and paisley" category of "just pretty designs".

Vessel SW1391a (see photo 75) of the Fourmile type, A.D. 1325-1400 (Carlson 1970:77) figures the "pueblo" icon on a hill surrounded by the icon for "earth/land". This is a common combination. Vessel SW1003 (see photo 76) of the Tularosa style A.D. 1200-1300 (Carlson 1970:91) is a very similar depiction. The only difference is that two "pueblo" icons are present and the hill is absent. QrPi20 (see photo 77) is a vessel which again exhibits the "pueblo" glyph, accompanied by the "earth/land" icon. Vessel SW1012 (see photo 78) is another example from the Raven Site Ruin which illustrates the "pueblo" glyph. This example includes the glyphs for "hill, geographic place, house/marriage, and earth/land". This representation varies slightly from the standard "pueblo" icon in that the "house/marriage" terraced units are not interlocked.

The American sign language gesture for "town" is nearly identical to the prehistoric icon of "pueblo". The gesture is performed by visually duplicating the roofs of many houses as seen from above (see figure 90). The only dissimilarity between the two is that the modern gesture duplicates the peaked roofs of modern buildings, and the prehistoric icon duplicates the terracing of the prehistoric pueblos. Among the Mandans and Arikaras during the nineteenth century, the sign language gesture for village was performed by placing the forefinger and thumb of each hand opposite each other as if to make a circle, but leaving between them a small interval; afterward move them from above downward simultaneously. The villages of both the Mandan and the Arikaras were fortified with a circular stockade, the gap between the thumb and forefinger represents the entrance/exit. Here again, the sign language gesture duplicates the physical attributes of the object or idea being represented.

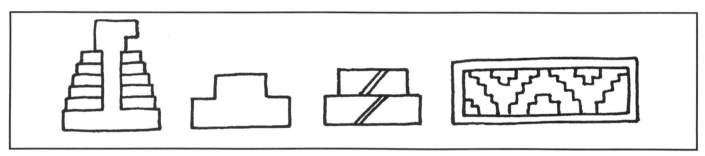

Figure 88. Use of terracing to depict buildings. (From Martineau 1987)

Figure 89. Petroglyph, Puerco River, Arizona. (From Barnes 1982)

Photo 74. "Pueblo" or "house/clan" glyph with interlocked terraced units and connecting spirals. This unit is translated by the modern Hopi as representing "migration". Springerville, Arizona.

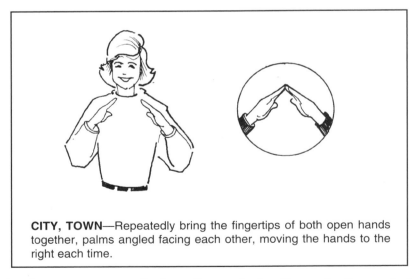

CITY, TOWN—Repeatedly bring the fingertips of both open hands together, palms angled facing each other, moving the hands to the right each time.

Fig. 90. The American sign language gesture for "town" reproducing the roofs of many buildings. (From Costello 1983:127)

Photo 75. SW1391a Fourmile Polychrome with a thunderbird flying over a " pueblo" glyph. (WMAC Collections)

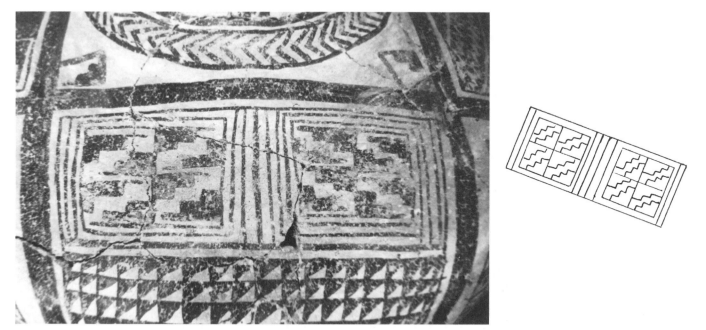

Photo 76. SW1003 Tularosa Black-on-white olla with two "pueblo" icons side by side. (WMAC Collections)

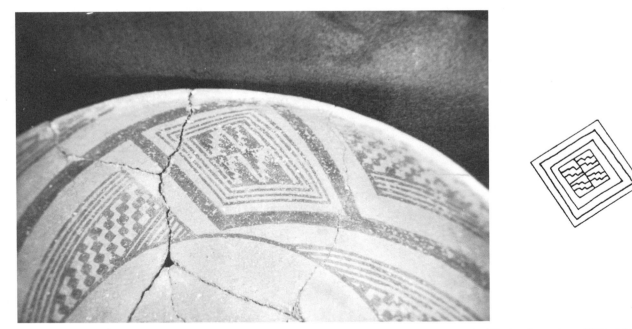

Photo 77. QrPi 20. Vessel showing the "pueblo" glyph. This example lacks the "hill" glyph as does SW1003 (see photo 76). (WMAC Collections)

Photo 78. Vessel SW1012 showing the "pueblo" glyph complete with "hill", "geographic place", "house/marriage", and "earth/land" icons. The "house/marriage" icons in this example are not interlocked, unless the white paint is intended to produce this effect. (WMAC Collections)

WAR

PEACE

The symbol for "war" consists of two symbols, i.e. two arrow points, touching. This produces an hourglass shaped icon. On petroglyphs and pictographs, and sometimes on pottery, the position of the icon will often reveal what was attacked, or what "war was made upon". The understanding of the positioning of symbols in relationship to one another is critical to their proper translation. If the "war" icon is touching another symbol, or the representation of a "real thing", i.e. a non-icon, than that is what "war was on" or what was under attack (see figure 91.) An excellent example of the "war" icon as a petroglyph can be seen near Three Rivers, New Mexico, reproduced in figure 92. A remarkably similar example illustrated on a Salado Polychrome vessel follows in photo 79.

Figure 93 is reproduced here to illustrate how universal the icon seems to be with protohistoric tribes. The Dakota, Delaware, Hopi, Aztec, and Pima all utilized the icon. From a world view, the "war" icon was also used by the Sumerians to mean "hostility" or "revolt".

There are several other examples of the "war" icon in the White Mountain Archaeological Center's collections. Vessel Pi5 (see photo 80) is a Gila Polychrome A.D. 1300-1600 (Cordell 1984:339) and it boldly exhibits the war symbol. Included in the layout of this vessel are other icons which are superimposed on the "war" icon. A white or negative circle is on each of the arrow points, i.e. each half of the "war" icon, and in the center of the white circle there is a cross. This is a reduced version of the White Mountains icon meaning "divide". The White Mountains glyph would include a dot in each of the quadrants created by the cross. The opposing panels include icons for "hill", "house/village (reduced form)", "earth/land" (see individual translations and vessel translation Pi5).

Vessel Pi22 (see photo 81) is totally covered with the "war" icon. The exterior of the bowl has eleven large "war" icons filled with the parallel lines indicating "earth/land". This may indicate that the war was about land or crops. The interior of the bowl with the exception of the center is filled

with the "war" icon in staggered pairs connected at the lateral tips of the arrow points. The interior layout brings us to a very interesting design element used by the prehistoric craftswomen to clarify individual icons and eliminate the confusion inherent with the constant presence of the negative patterns. If the "war" icon is linked side by side, the negative design element created is the "peace" icon, i.e. linked diamonds (see figure 94 and photo 82). The author of this vessel deliberately obliterated the "peace" icon by creating pairs of the "war" icon and staggering the pairs so that the opposite "peace" symbol would not appear. If any more than two "war" icons are joined, the negative "peace" symbol is created. Similarly, on the exterior of the same bowl, the "war" icons are not touching, thereby not creating the opposite "peace" icon. The woman who painted this vessel wanted no ambiguity.

An example of another technique used to clarify which icon to read, positive or negative, can be seen on vessel SW1003 (see photo 82). On this vessel the "war" icon is the negative, but ironically the negative is the painted portion, the black. How can this be? When the artist painted the olla, she placed dots in the "peace" icons, which indicates that this is the icon which should catch your eye, and this probably indicates that this glyph should be read FIRST. If both icons are present (in this case "war" and "peace") then both icons are relevant to the overall meaning of the vessel. The inclusion of the dot pulls your eye to the first icon to read, in this case "peace". You then secondarily see the negative "war" icon, quite literally between the lines. The use of the dot to draw attention to a symbol is prevalent on many pottery vessels where a confusion between positive and negative glyphs may otherwise occur.

The Mimbres potters carried the use of mixed positive and negative imagery to extremes with depictions that are often difficult to differentiate. Figure 95 shows just one example of a Classic Mimbres Black-on-white bowl where the positive and negative imagery is so perfectly blended, that at first glance your eye is confused. Even after closer examination of this bowl it is still perplexing. This is undoubtedly deliberate.

The hourglass "war" icon is a carryover from the prehistoric pueblo people of the Southwest to the Athapaskan speakers who arrived from the north in the sixteenth century (Cordell 1984). In Navajo mythology, the war twins are the children of the sun and Changing Woman (Reichard 1950) and are called Monster Slayer and Born-for-Water. These deities can be found on examples of eighteenth century rock art (see figure 96). Superimposed on these representations are the hourglass "war" icons. This icon can also be found on the painted masks and on the ceremonial impersonators of Born-for-Water (Schaafsma 1980). In prehistoric pueblo rock art, the symbol for "war" can be found pecked on representations of warriors (see figure 97).

A possible personification of the "war" icon to create the icon "warrior" may be seen in figure 98.

The body shape of the anthromorph in the petroglyph is without a doubt the "war" icon, and the addition of the head, arms, and legs complete the glyph. An alternate interpretation of the hourglass anthropomorphic figure is presented by LaVan Martineau (1973). He argues that hourglass anthromorphs, and even occasionally zoomorphs, represent, in some cases, "starvation". Physical affliction is depicted in proto-historic symbolism of the North American Indians. Smallpox is represented by dots, and stomach ailments by spirals on the abdomen (Mallery 1879-80) and this possibility should not be disregarded.

The American sign language gesture for "to defend or guard against" is reproduced in figure 99 and is gesturally a match to the "war" icon. The sign language gesture for "peace" is shown in figure 100, and it creates the linked diamonds of the prehistoric glyph. (Costello 1983, Butterworth and Flodin 1983).

Figure 91. A protohistoric petroglyphic panel depicting Kit Carson's Navajo campaign of 1863-64. The "war" icon appears in several places. It is attached to a "corn" glyph (center left) indicating that the corn was destroyed. (From Martineau 1973).

Figure 92. Petroglyph, Three Rivers, New Mexico showing the "war" icon. (From Martineau 1973:106).

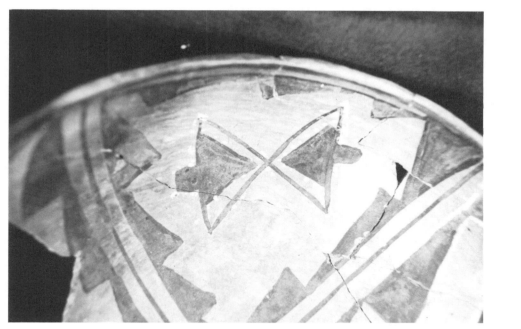
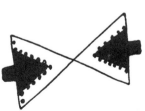

Photo 79. Vessel Qr79, Salado Polychrome bowl showing a tilted "war" icon. The white dots within the glyph may represent "water". (WMAC Collections)

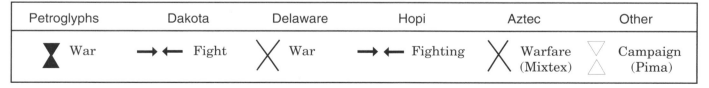

Petroglyphs	Dakota	Delaware	Hopi	Aztec	Other
War	→ ← Fight	⚔ War	→ ← Fighting	⚔ Warfare (Mixtex)	▽ Campaign (Pima) △

Figure 93. Proto-historic and prehistoric groups that utilized the "war" icon. (From Martineau 1973:138).

Figure 94. "War" icon in positive and the linked diamond "peace" icon in negative.

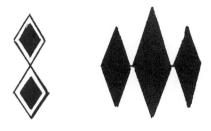

Figure 94a. "Peace" icons found on Apache and Washoe baskets. (From Martineau 1973)

Photo 80. Vessel Pi5, a Gila Polychrome bowl dating from A.D. 1300-1600 (Cordell 1984) with a large "war" icon at center. (WMAC Collections)

Photo 81. Vessel Pi22, showing the "war" icon on the exterior and interior. Exterior includes the icon for "earth/land" and the interior icon is deliberately arranged to obliterate the possible negative "peace" symbol. (WMAC Collections)

Photo 82. Vessel SW1003 a Tularosa Black-on-white olla dating A.D. 1200-1300 (Carlson 1970). The "peace" icon in the negative contains the eye-catching dot at center, indicating that "peace" should be read first. The "war" icon is in positive but becomes the background. (WMAC Collections)

Figure 95. Mimbres Classic Black-on-white, Style III, using positive and negative imagery to create two perfectly blended sets of images. Dagny Janss, Los Angeles. (From Brody 1983)

Figure 96. Navajo supernaturals the "warrior twins", Born-For-Water and Monster Slayer, with the "war" icon scratched through the paint. Largo Canyon Drainage, New Mexico. (From Schaafsma 1980)

Figure 97. Teakwaina kachina, Second Mesa showing the "war" icon superimposed. (From Schaafsma 1980)

Figure 98. Petroglyph in the Gila style from South Mountains, Arizona, showing the "war" icon with anthropomorphic features, possibly representing "warrior". (From Schaafsma 1980)

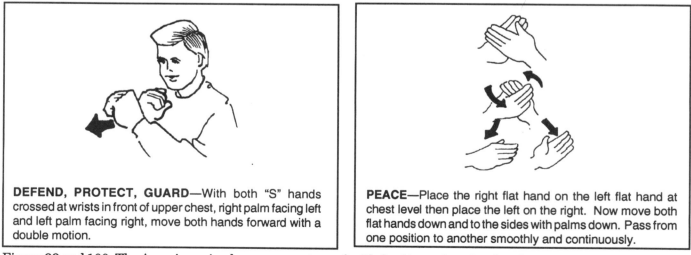

DEFEND, PROTECT, GUARD—With both "S" hands crossed at wrists in front of upper chest, right palm facing left and left palm facing right, move both hands forward with a double motion.

PEACE—Place the right flat hand on the left flat hand at chest level then place the left on the right. Now move both flat hands down and to the sides with palms down. Pass from one position to another smoothly and continuously.

Figure 99 and 100. The American sign language gestures for "defend/guard against" and "peace" (From Butterworth and Flodin 1983) (Costello 1983)

WATER/RAIN

The icon found on prehistoric Southwest pottery that represents "water/rain" is most usually comprised of a series of dots. These dots most likely represent the falling droplets of rain. Often "water/rain" is symbolized by hatchure lines, representing the path of the falling rain, and on occasion ticking along the edges of another icon may represent water. Dots representing droplets of water or "wet" are also found on petroglyphs in the Southwest. Another common petroglyph and pictograph representation is the "cupped hand" glyph, although this symbol is less identifiable on pottery. It is an exact match to the North American Indian sign language gesture (Mallery 1879-80:494) (see figure 101).

Falling rain could almost be discussed as a separate icon. It is represented frequently and examples are abundant. Without surprise it is often found in conjunction with the "cloud" and "wind" icon families. Examples include:

Qr15, a Salado Polychrome thunderstorm effigy, showing falling rain as hatchure lines under the icon for "cloud" (see photo 83).

SW1013, a Fourmile Polychrome dating A.D. 1325-1400 (Carlson 1970) showing falling rain as droplets between parallel lines almost resembling the notes of a musical scale. This representation could mean "rain falling onto the earth", the earth represented as parallel lines (see icon for "earth/land"). (see photo 84).

SW1003, a Tularosa Black-on-white olla, dating A.D. 1200-1300 (Carlson 1970: 91) showing falling rain very graphically as dots falling from the sky between the icon for "mountain" (see "Mountains"). This representation could possibly be "snow", however, no other examples have as yet been discovered for comparison. (see photo 85).

Rain cloud patterns and falling rain are also found on both Hopi and Zuni kachinas, (see figure 102 and 103).

From a world view, the Egyptians and Chinese also represented the falling rain with the "cloud" icon (see figure 104). The "water/rain" icon is frequently found with other weather elements such as "wind" and "clouds". These representations are very common, and are combined in every possible way. The frequency of combinations of weather elements surrounding the "water/rain" icon is not surprising in the marginal environment of the Southwest. If the rains did not come, people starved, water being the single most critical resource for the population (Cordell 1984: 2). Water/rain was important to the prehistoric Southwest Indian, consequentially they used the various icons frequently. One is reminded of the many names and combinations of meanings that the Inuit have for "snow" for precisely the same reason, that is, it's important to them. Examples of weather element combinations including the "water/rain" icon include:

Qr83, Gila Polychrome vessel showing "water/rain" dots in combination with the "wind" icon. (see photo 86).

SW1508, Tonto Polychrome vessel with the "water/rain" icon in combination with "cloud" and "wind". (see photo 87).

SW1013, Fourmile Polychrome vessel showing the "water/rain" icon in conjunction with "clouds" and "wind" icons. (see photo 88).

The use of dots to represent "water/rain" is also revealed on the rain bringing thunderbird of vessel SW1391a. The dots are found on his "arrow" icon head, within his body and in conjunction with the "will not be turned away" or "rain streamer" icon trailing his flight. (see photo 89 and the translation of SW1391a).

A nearly identical vessel was excavated by J. Walter Fewkes in 1895 (see figure 105). This rain bringing thunderbird also exhibits the "water/rain" icon as dots along the margins of the head.

Certainly not all rows of dots on all pottery vessels necessarily represent the "water/rain" icon, some must certainly fall into the "pretty pattern" category. However, when the icon is used in relevant conjunction with other symbols, the meaning of the "water/rain" icon is undeniable.

An example of ticking along the edge of another icon to represent "water/rain" is found on vessel SW1013. The overall translation of this bowl con-

Photo 83. Vessel Qr15, thunderstorm effigy showing "falling rain" as hatchure lines below the "cloud" icon. (WMAC Collections)

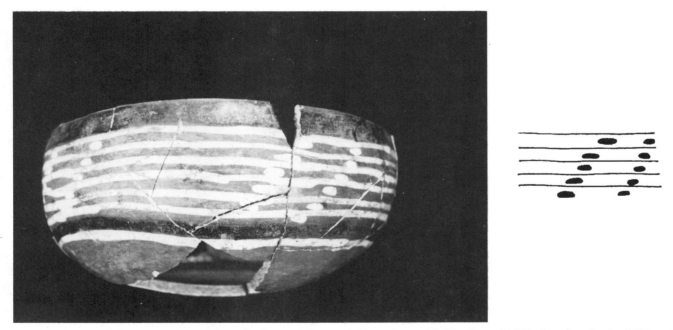

Photo 84. Vessel SW1013 Fourmile Polychrome dating A.D. 1325-1400 (Carlson 1970) showing "rain falling to the earth". (WMAC Collections)

cludes that, at least in this instance, the ticking does represent "water/rain" (see translations vessel SW1013, photo 90.) One last combination using the "water/rain" icon that is found commonly on prehistoric Southwest pottery is the union of a row of dots along a row of parallel lines. The two icons involved are the "water/rain" icon and the "earth/land" icon. This combination could mean "watered earth" or "rain fallen on the earth". Examples of this combination include vessel SW1028 (see photo 91) and sherds from room 18 at Raven Site Ruin (photo 92). An even more persuasive example is vessel SW1013 (see photo 84). As mentioned with the "falling rain" combinations, this vessel exhibits dots in between rows of parallel lines, demonstrating "rain falling onto watered land". It includes not only the "water/rain" icon and the "earth/land" icon, but combines them in a manner to demonstrate the rain actually falling onto the earth.

Two examples from Mexico (see figure 106) include "drinking" showing the water droplets brought to the mouth, and the symbol for "rain" showing the water droplets falling to earth (Mallery 1879-80:357).

The American sign language gestures for "wet" and "rain falling" are reproduced in figures 107 and 108. Similarity to the prehistoric icons is evident, the fingers reproducing the path of the falling rain and the closed hands at the end of the "wet" gesture being similar to the many dots used to symbolically represent the idea of "wet" prehistorically. The American Indian sign language gesture is reproduced in figure 109. It is identical to the gesture used today.

No other icon is so utilized on prehistoric Southwest pottery as the "water/rain" representations and the weather elements that accompany them. Water, or the lack of water, to a prehistoric Southwest Indian was a life or death situation. As soon as hunting and gathering was overshadowed by sedentary villages and dependency on farming, the rains became critical. This urgency is reflected on the patterns and iconographic combinations seen on a majority of decorated pottery vessels from at least as early as A.D. 1200 and continuing until A.D. 1400 and possibly as late as A.D. 1450 in the area of the Little Colorado Plateau.

Photo 85. Vessel SW1003 showing rain falling. This representation could be "snow". (WMAC Collections)

Figure 101. The cupped hand glyph representing "water" (From Martineau 1987:26). This icon is less common on pottery than on petroglyphs.

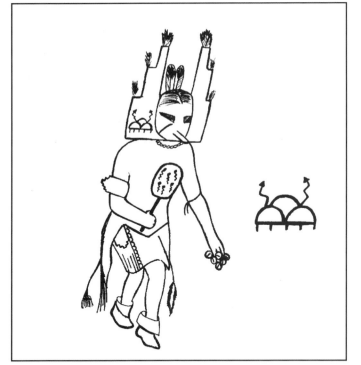

Figure 102. Hopi Kachina "Kaqaika'a" showing falling "rain" icon combined with "cloud" and "lightning" symbols. (From Wright 1973:195).

Figure 103. Zuni Kachina "Wamuwe" showing "falling rain" icon in association with "clouds" (From Wright 1985: 113).

Figure 104. North American Indian, Egyptian, Chinese symbols showing "falling rain". (From Martineau 1987:152)

Photo 86. Vessel Qr83 "water/rain" icon combined with "wind" icon. (WMAC Collections)

Photo 87. SW1508 Tonto Polychrome showing "water/rain" icon combined with "cloud" and "wind" icons. (WMAC Collections)

Photo 88. Vessel SW1013 Fourmile Polychrome with "water/rain" icon combined with "clouds" and "wind". (WMAC Collections)

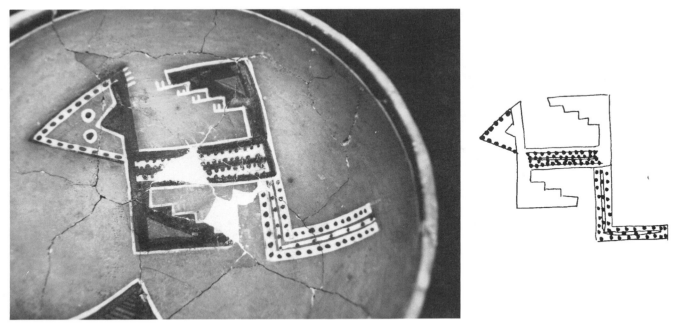

Photo 89. Vessel SW1391a Fourmile Polychrome with thunderbird. "Water/rain" icon is represented by dots on the margins of the "arrow" head, within the body and within the trailing icon. (WMAC Collections)

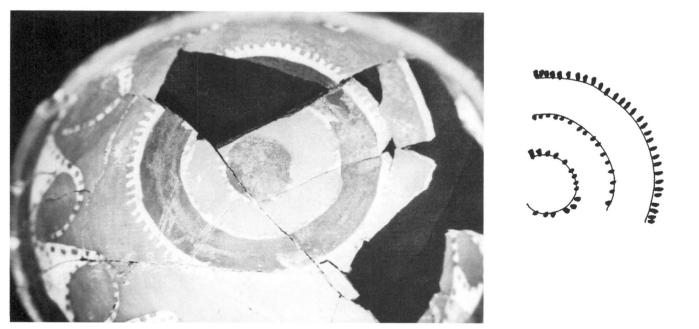

Photo 90. Vessel SW1013 Fourmile Polychrome. Vessel exhibits ticking on the margins of another icon, demonstrating the "water/rain" symbol. (WMAC Collections)

Figure 105. Sikyatki vessel with thunderbird. "Water/rain" icon is represented as in photo 89 with dots on the margin of the head. (From Fewkes 1895:169)

Figure 106. Mexican pictograph showing "to drink" and "rain", both symbols using the water droplet representation (From Mallery 1879 80:357)

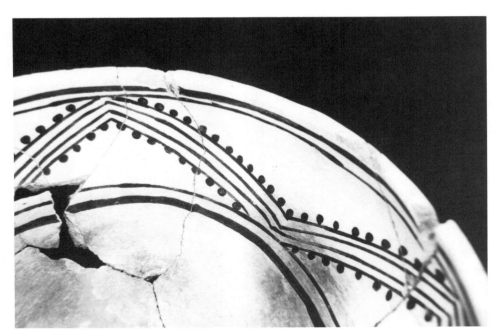
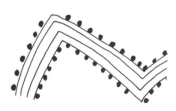

Photo 91. SW1028 "watered earth" combination. Dots representing the "water/rain" icon combined with the icon for "earth/land". (WMAC Collections)

Photo 92. Sherds from room #18, Raven Site Ruin, Springerville, Arizona showing the "watered earth" icon combination. (WMAC Collections)

Photo 92a. Petroglyph showing "descending water". The spiral indicates "ascend or descend" and the wavy line indicates the water running downward. Behind the rock displaying the glyph, a spring runs down to the river below. The spiral and the water glyph are touching. This positioning is a determinative, or key sign, an unspoken but understood indicator to read both glyphs together. Springerville, Arizona.

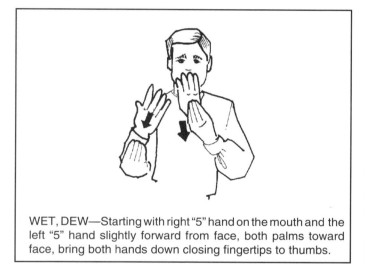

WET, DEW—Starting with right "5" hand on the mouth and the left "5" hand slightly forward from face, both palms toward face, bring both hands down closing fingertips to thumbs.

Figure 107. The American sign language gesture for "wet", the closed fingers reproducing the water droplet idea. (From Costello 1983)

RAIN—Bring both loose "claw" hands, palms down, starting at shoulder level, down twice with deliberate movement.

Figure 108. American sign language representation for "falling rain". (From Costello 1983; 120)

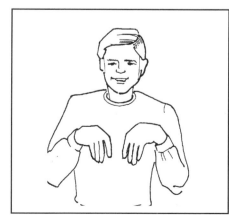

Figure 109. The Shoshoni, Apache, et al. sign language for "falling rain", is identical to the modern gesture. (From Mallery 1879-80:344)

WIND, SMOKE, MOTION

The prehistoric Indian icon that represents "wind" on the pottery vessels is a tapering spiral. The spiral in isolation of other icons means only "motion", but when combined with other glyphs it can often represent "wind" or even "smoke". These icons are often complete with rain symbols which are usually dots representing the water droplets or short hatchure lines representing the path of the falling rain (see "water/rain"). The icon for wind was long confused as a possible icon for "cloud" because both are depicted in conjunction with other weather elements. "Cloud" icons are always depicted with more mass than "wind" icons. "Wind" is a narrow swirling, tapering spiral, whereas "clouds" are terraced, bulky, domed icons often resembling mountains (see "Clouds" and "Mountains").

Two excellent examples of the "wind" icon in context are vessels Qr15 and SW1013. Qr15 (see photo 93) demonstrates the wind during a thunderstorm, one set of spirals is solid and the other is complete with hatchured lines representing falling rain. Vessel SW1013 (see photo 94) is a Fourmile Polychrome bowl (Carlson 1970) bordered on the inside surface just below the rim with the "wind" icon in conjunction with the "rain" symbol.

The "wind" icon is abundant on prehistoric pottery, so abundant as to be a favorite filler pattern, and lose its meaning falling into the plaid and paisley category of "just pretty designs". This is especially true of Tularosa material. The interlocked spirals are used as a diagnostic trait of the pottery type. Gila and Tonto Polychrome vessels also often display the "wind" icon, although its meaning may be lost and only its aesthetic value utilized (see Vessels; SW1508, photo 95, Qr83, photo 96).

An interesting similarity or possible confusion exists between the "wind" icon and the icon for "smoke". Figure 111 shows a Casas Grandes Villa Ahumada Polychrome effigy vessel of "the smoker" (Moulard 1984, plate 81) with a "hiculi" or peyote spiral on top of his head which is thought to represent the swirling smoke produced by his pipe. This may well be the case, the motion of swirling smoke and swirling wind is not contradictory. This "hiculi" symbol on top of his head is complete with a water symbol, i.e. the ticking along the edges of the icon. The smoker also has lightning bolts displayed on his shins and bullseye water dots down his arms. Could the smoker be involved in a rain prayer ritual? Smoking is associated at Casas Grandes with shamanism and curing (Moulard 1984). Among the Huichol of Mexico, the plain spiral is associated with snakes and water and the ticked spiral with the use of peyote during prayer. The pilgrimage to obtain peyote is coordinated with the coming of the rains (Mountjoy 1974).

The modern American sign language gesture for "wind" depicts the motion of the wind as does the prehistoric icon. A better correlation is seen when the prehistoric "wind" icon is compared to the sign language gesture for "tornado". This correlation is even better appreciated by natives of the Southwest who have experienced the excitement and discomfort of the region's August "dust devils". The North American Indian sign language gesture for both "wind" and "smoke" depict the motion of the swirling air (Mallery 1879-80), as does the modern American sign language gesture.

Figure 110. Petroglyph from Dinosaur National Park, Utah, showing depiction of a "whirlwind". (Schaafsma 1980)

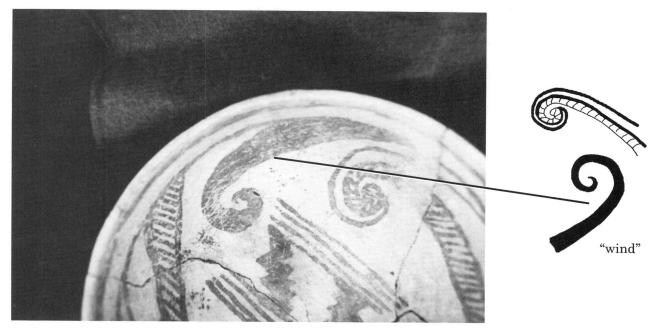

"wind"

Photo 93. Qr15 Thunderstorm vessel showing "wind" icon and "cloud" with "falling rain" hatchures. Salado Polychrome. (WMAC Collections)

Photo 94. SW1013 Fourmile Polychrome bowl with "wind" and "rain" icon dating A.D. 1325-1400 (WMAC Collections)

Photo 95. SW1508 Tonto Polychrome vessel showing "wind", "rain", and "cloud" icons in association. Because of this combination of the weather elements, the individual meanings of the icons are unmistakable. Excavated at Raven Site Ruin, Springerville, Arizona. (WMAC Collections)

Photo 96. Qr83 Gila Polychrome vessel with "wind" icon and "rain" icon incorporated. (WMAC Collections)

Figure 111. Villa Ahumada Polychrome effigy with "hiculi" spiral on top of his head, representing "smoke?", "wind with rain?", or "smoker praying for rain?" Notice the lightning icons on the shins and the "rain/water" icons down each arm. (From Moulard 1984)

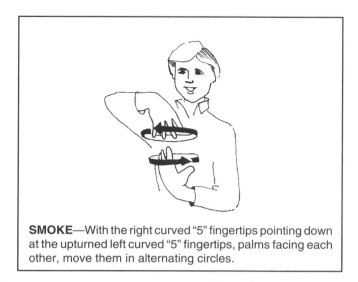

SMOKE—With the right curved "5" fingertips pointing down at the upturned left curved "5" fingertips, palms facing each other, move them in alternating circles.

Figure 112. The American sign language gesture for "smoke" (From Costello 1983:154). Like "wind" it reproduces the movements associated with both as does the proto-historic gesture used by the North American Indians.

Archaeologist Jeff Brown stabilizing a doorway. Room 31, South Pueblo, Raven Site Ruin.

Over 70 different ceramic types have been discovered at Raven Site Ruin including Cibola whitewares, White Mountain redwares and Zuni glazewares.

Screening room 9. The north pueblo at Raven Site Ruin suffered extensive damage from looters making analyzing and stabilizing a monumental project.

Ceramic cluster between south wall and mealing bins. Room 31, South Pueblo, Raven Site Ruin.

Chapter IV

Prehistoric Ceramic Icons as Compared to Modern Sign Language

Chart III

Translation	Prehistoric Icon	Modern Signing
Arrow point. Hurt, harm, attack. Will cause harm/Will not cause harm (dependent upon direction of the point).		**HURT, PAIN, ACHE, SORE—** Jab the extended index finger-tips toward each other in front of body several times without making contact with each other, palms facing chest. Note: Can be signed near the point of pain.
Cloud.		**CLOUD**—With loose "claw" hands, palms forward above shoulder level, move hands in outward arcs ending with palms facing body.
Corn.		**CORN**—The extended left index finger points forward, representing the corncob, while the right thumb and index finger rub back and forth along the finger, as if scraping off kernels.
Death/die.		**DEATH, DEAD, DIE, EXPIRE, PERISH**—Hold both flat hands to the front with the right palm facing up and the left palm facing down. Move both hands in an arc to the left while changing the hand positions so that the palms reverse direction.
Divide/divided.		**DIVIDE**—With the right "b" hand on top of the left "b" hand, both palms facing each other and fingers pointing forward and angled inward, move the hands downward and apart.
Earth/land/rows of crops.		**LAND, FIELD**—Rub the thumbs of both hands across the fingertips from the little finger to the index finger. Push both downturned "5" hands forward and outward, fingers pointing forward.

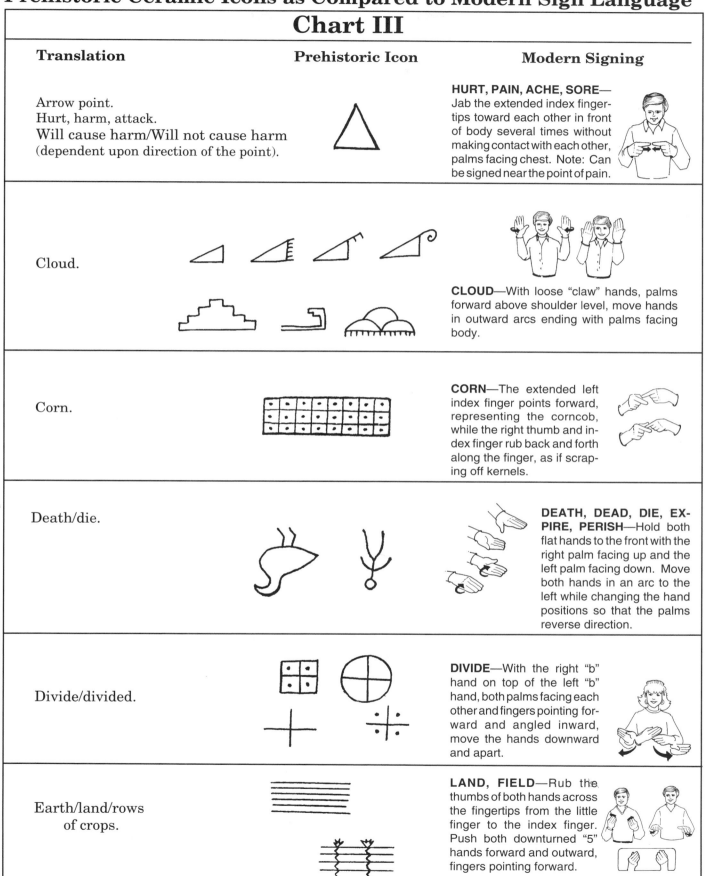

Translation	Prehistoric Icon	Modern Signing
Far. Distant.		**FAR—** Hands are held together, thumbs pointing away from the body. The right hand moves straight ahead in a slight arc. The left hand does not move.
Fly. Flight.		**FLY—**With the right extended thumb, index finger and little finger, palm down, above the right shoulder, move the hand forward.
Four directions.		**DIRECTION—**Move both "d" hands, palms facing each other and index fingers pointing forward, back and forth in front of the body in alternating movements.
Heaven. House in the clouds. Entrance to the spiritual realm.		**HEAVEN—**Both open hands, fingers straight and pointing up, move upward in an arc on either side of the head. Just before they touch above the head, the right hand, palm down, sweeps under the left and moves up, its palm now facing out.
House. Marriage.		**HOUSE—**Start with touching index fingertips of angled "b" hands at the forehead, palms down. Separate, bringing hands downward at an angle to shoulder width, then straight down, palms facing. **MARRY—**Bring both slightly curved open hands, palms facing each other at an angle, together and clasp.

Translation	Prehistoric Icon	Modern Signing
Lightning.		**LIGHTNING**—Make quick jagged downward movements with the right index finger.
Mountain. Hill.		**MOUNTAIN, HILL**—Strike the closed right hand on the back of the closed left hand (the sign for rock), then move both open hands upward to the front with a wavy motion.
Peace.		**PEACE**—Place the right flat hand on the left flat hand at chest level; then place the left on the right. Now move both flat hands down and to the sides with palms down. Pass from one position to another smoothly and continuously.
Place. Geographic area.		**PLACE**—(The letter "P"; a circle or square is indicated, to show the locale or place.) The "P" hands are held side by side before the body, with middle fingertips touching. From this position, the hands separate and outline a circle (or a square) before coming together again closer to the body.
Pueblo. Village. Town.		**CITY, TOWN**—Repeatedly bring the fingertips of both open hands together, palms angled facing each other, moving the hands to the right each time.
Rain. Rain falling.		**RAIN**—Bring both loose "claw" hands, palms down, starting at shoulder level, down twice with deliberate movement.

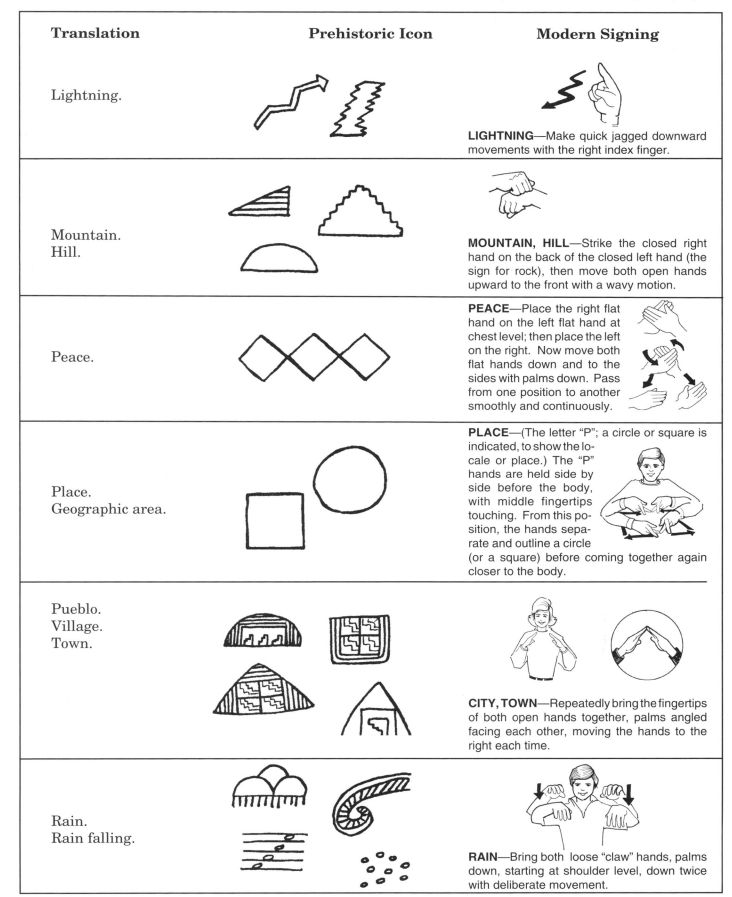

Translation	Prehistoric Icon	Modern Signing

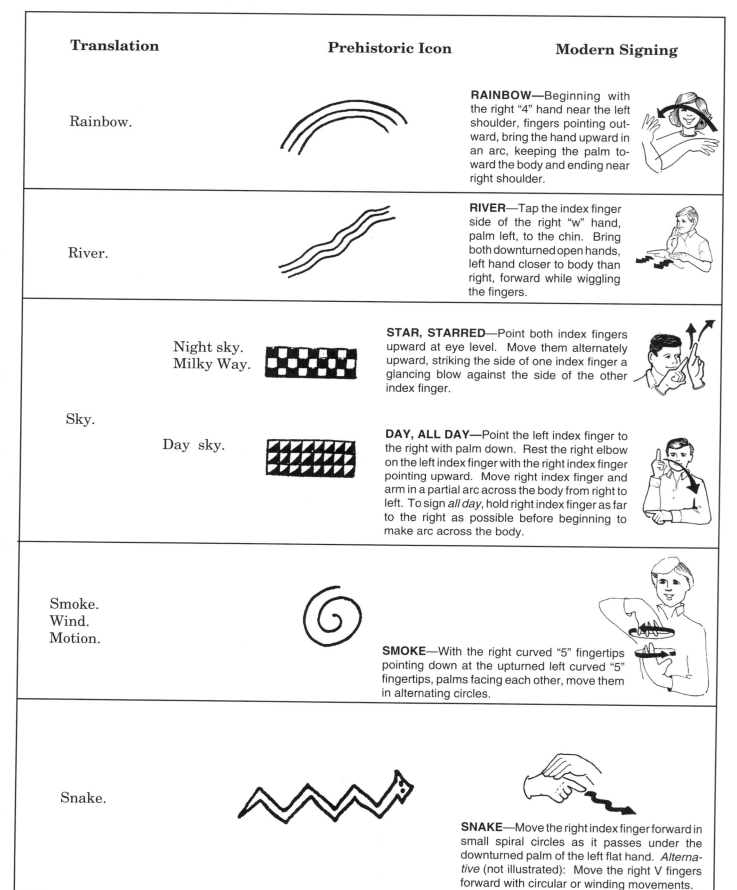

Rainbow.

RAINBOW—Beginning with the right "4" hand near the left shoulder, fingers pointing outward, bring the hand upward in an arc, keeping the palm toward the body and ending near right shoulder.

River.

RIVER—Tap the index finger side of the right "w" hand, palm left, to the chin. Bring both downturned open hands, left hand closer to body than right, forward while wiggling the fingers.

Sky.

Night sky.
Milky Way.

STAR, STARRED—Point both index fingers upward at eye level. Move them alternately upward, striking the side of one index finger a glancing blow against the side of the other index finger.

Day sky.

DAY, ALL DAY—Point the left index finger to the right with palm down. Rest the right elbow on the left index finger with the right index finger pointing upward. Move right index finger and arm in a partial arc across the body from right to left. To sign *all day*, hold right index finger as far to the right as possible before beginning to make arc across the body.

Smoke.
Wind.
Motion.

SMOKE—With the right curved "5" fingertips pointing down at the upturned left curved "5" fingertips, palms facing each other, move them in alternating circles.

Snake.

SNAKE—Move the right index finger forward in small spiral circles as it passes under the downturned palm of the left flat hand. *Alternative* (not illustrated): Move the right V fingers forward with circular or winding movements.

Translation	Prehistoric Icon	Modern Signing
Something. Something there.		**SOMEONE, SOMEBODY, SOMETHING**—With the extended index finger pointing upward, palm facing out, make a small circle in the air with the whole arm and repeat movement.
Tension. Stress. Fear. Confusion.		**FEAR, CONFUSION**—Start with both raised hands held on left side of body, left held higher than right, palms facing outward. Move both hands downward simultaneously with wavy motions.
Water. Wet.		**WET, DEW**—Starting with right "5" hand on the mouth and the left "5" hand slightly forward from face, both palms toward face, bring both hands down closing fingertips to thumbs.
War.		**DEFEND, GUARD, PROTECT**—With both hands crossed at wrists in front of upper chest, right palm facing left and left palm facing right, move both hands forward with a double motion.
Wind.		**WIND, BREEZE**—Starting with both "5" hands, fingers pointing right, right palm toward chest and left palm forward, bring hands across in front of body repeatedly, reversing hand positions on opposite side of body. **TORNADO**—Starting with the right index finger near and pointing down to the left index finger, pointing up, spiral the right fingertip away in an upward motion.

Chapter V

Summary and Conclusions

From the temporal period beginning perhaps as early as A.D. 1200 with the appearance of the Tularosa Black-on-white ceramic types and continuing to A.D. 1400 and possibly even as late as A.D. 1450, in the area of the White Mountains in East/Central Arizona, the painted representations found on ceramics are more than "just pretty designs". From the Tularosa phase and through the Fourmile Polychrome period ceramic vessel production, symbols were used on pottery to illustrate narratives and to relate information. These symbols when presented alone contain a recognized unit meaning. When they are combined, used in multiples and positioned in relation to each other, they create larger bodies of information. The recognition of these symbols and their meaning went far beyond the immediate White Mountains area. This iconography often in a reduced form has been found to the south below the Mogollon Rim as demonstrated by the iconography of the Salado and Gila Polychromes, and to the northern pueblos where its reflection may survive in the Katsina cults to this day. This is not to say that these areas are the only places in the Southwest where iconography was employed. There may be many others remaining to be recognized.

It is possible that the development of the White Mountains fine Polychrome pottery helped stimulate the use of iconography on the vessels being made. In the Mimbres Valley, the development of the Classic Black-on-white vessels around A.D. 1000, along with the vessel's use in mortuary practices, may have resulted in the array of realism (realism for the Mimbrenos) blended with a smattering of iconography that is found on the ceramics of the period. The development of the ceramic technology was probably at least partly responsible for the advancement of the application of the iconographic symbols. Egyptian hieroglyphs became a flowing, realistically presented script because of their application on papyrus. They became more graphic, just as cuneiform became a nongraphic, standardized, rigid form with the use of the restrictive stylus in the media of wet clay. In the Southwest, the bright colors and high quality of the glazes coupled with the detailed execution resulted in the beginning of something much larger than just attractive ceramics. The media allowed the artist the freedom to say more.

The discovery of an icon in isolation is far more difficult to translate than one found in conjunction with other symbols. It is usually the context of the icon that aids in the translation. This use of icons in combination is an obvious advantage in translating the iconography found on ceramics, as opposed to the iconography found on petroglyphs or pictographs. With the rock art of the Southwest, the symbols are layered. It is difficult if not impossible to tell who carved or painted what and when. With these layers of rock art it is difficult to determine the relationship between symbols. The only time these relationships can be discussed is in the rare case when the rock art is devoid of more recent markings than the original artist intended, or when the stylistics or technique of the two or more artists separated by time are obvious enough to warrant their differentiation. With a ceramic bowl or jar, this problem does not exist. These vessels were created by one craftswoman, during one temporal period. Not only do the relationships between icons display relevancy, but they also demonstrate something about how that one woman saw the world around her and how she translated what she saw into the recognized symbolism of her day.

One of the inherent advantages of finding icons on prehistoric ceramics is the verification of that particular symbol's use during the production of that particular pottery type. Pottery typology in the Southwest is a primary vehicle to the determination of a calendar date, often to within fifty years of accuracy. Because of the abundance of pottery found in the sites of the Southwest, this methodology has been used practically as long as archaeology has been a recognized science.

The first use of symbolism found on ceramics in a combined and meaningful way in the White Mountains area seems to be the early Tularosa period at about A.D. 1200. Most Tularosa material displays no meaningful iconography, at least not any that is presented clearly enough for modern translation. Occasionally, in what seem to be isolated bursts, symbols begin to appear and vessels blossom with meaning. It is not the norm, but the chance discovery of these ceramic pieces result in the interpretation of symbols previously unknown. As the ceramic tradition progresses, the symbols become more frequent and standardized. With the advent of the Fourmile Polychromes, from about A.D. 1325 to A.D. 1400 and possibly as late as A.D. 1450 in the heart of the White Mountains, iconography is full blown. Symbols are combined into complex scenarios and glyphs are blended into combined secondary and even tertiary meanings. The icons during this Fourmile period are complex. A single idea may contain four or five individual parts to clarify the whole. For example, the glyph for "pueblo/town" during this period consists of the symbol for "hill", "earth/land", "property/geographic place", and four interlocked "house/marriage" units. These early and very graphic depictions are wonderfully informative and essential to the translation of later glyphs. Toward the end of the Fourmile period, evidence of symbol reduction begins to appear. This reduction is also seen in the Salado and Gila Polychromes to the south of the White Mountains area. Icons that were previously complex, utilizing up to four individual symbols, are now painted with only two of the necessary elements to relate the meaning of the glyph. The icons are still combined in meaningful relationships, the symbols still retain their recognized meanings, but the execution is simpler. This would seem to indicate that these symbols are more widely understood. They are no longer isolated to one region. The White Mountain area along the Little Colorado River and the river valleys below the Mogollon Rim are two distinct groups separated by distance and culture. With the spread of iconography to the south, the symbols no longer require all of the elements previously contained in the glyph for the

meaning to be clear. It is possible that these changes were the result of cultural differences between the northern White Mountains area and the Salados to the south, or perhaps the simplification was utilized in order to put more information onto one vessel. One is reminded of the deterioration of Roman coinage with its use distant from the source. The greater the distance from Rome, the greater the distortion of the symbols, dates and figures. In the White Mountains, with the coming of the vitreous Zuni glazes of 1450 A.D., the use of icons in that area is virtually extinct. Occasionally mixed with the later Zuni material, a Gila Polychrome traded from the south will appear with a smattering of iconography, but most of the symbolism is lost. It could be possible that a migration of the Little Colorado people to the south to the area below the Mogollon Rim resulted in the use of iconography in that area. The termination of meaningful symbolism in the White Mountains area with the introduction of the Zuni glazes at 1450 A.D. and the continuation of the use of reduced iconography below the Mogollon Rim throughout the Gila Polychrome period, and even possibly into the Tonto Polychromes production, would lend some support to this idea. It is equally as likely that the iconography traveled to the South along the well established pochteca trade routes from the White Mountain area to the region below the Mogollon Rim, and that the White Mountain area culturally terminated for other reasons prior to A.D. 1400 was resettled by another cultural group after A.D. 1400, i. e. the appearance of the Zuni glazes, and that below the Mogollon Rim the culture, and subsequent icon use, simply continued undisrupted well into the fifteenth century.

Because a ceramic vessel can be accurately given a calendar date, these vessels have a tremendous advantage over rock art when considering iconography and the interpretation of culture.

When a symbol is discovered on a ceramic vessel, and when that symbol is correctly translated, the researcher gains an understanding for the first time of not only what represented what during a precise period of time, but also of how the members of this culture thought. The combination of icons to illustrate an event, or to relate a story or legend, tells us far more about the people who lived and died on a particular site than the splashy discovery of a cache of esoteric material from a kiva vault. Many of the narratives illustrated may in fact be accounts of prehistory. When I look at vessel SW1011 which illustrates a "siege", I genuinely wonder if that depiction is telling me the story of an actual attack that occurred between the years A.D. 1325 and A.D. 1400 on the actual hill where the bowl was found. If researchers begin to look at ceramic material with the possibility in mind that the symbols they are seeing are more than aesthetically pleasing, and that these icons could possibly have a real meaning that can be translated and used to help translate other symbols found on other ceramics, then we may be able to eventually interpret actual accounts of prehistory.

The material that has been presented here is going to cause the majority of researchers today to be highly critical. They will discount the possibility that modern sign language can be used to help interpret prehistoric glyphs. It is difficult to comprehend that modern signing would have any similarity to prehistoric signing and then to two dimensional glyphs, unless there were somehow a continuum from one to the next. These similarities exist because WE haven't changed all that much. The human animal is, in fact, the glue of the continuum. In the absence of speech, the gestures employed to relate ideas between human beings are very, very graphic. In the communicative vacuum before man learned to record his speech phonetically, the ideograms used two dimensionally are also very graphic.

Critics will also claim that the signing only matches the glyphs because I have forced a "fit" by creatively matching the sign language to the glyph or vice versa. The method used to translate an icon was first to examine the glyph in context. To view it in relation to other symbols, and try to determine what it was, i.e. what it means, by viewing first what it looks like, then its position and how it was used. The best evidence became the recognition of large complex glyphs which could be broken down into smaller units. This revealed several previously unknown icons. Often these larger glyphs were very graphic. In other words, they looked like what they were. The meaning of these smaller components within the larger glyph although simple, once they were viewed individually and in context, became distinct. It was only after these compari-

sons, and after comparing the suspected icon to other ethnographic material and the glyphs found on rock art, was the idea represented "looked up" in the various American sign language dictionaries. The gesture was often very similar to the icon. This is remarkable, but true. Often the match requires that you limit or expand your thinking to the context of the prehistoric Southwest. For example, the "earth/land" icon matches the modern American sign language gesture for "land". It does not match the modern gesture for "earth", because the modern gesture illustrates a round earth rotating on its axis. Prehistoric Indians probably did not know that the earth was round or that it rotated.

Not all of the icons exactly matched the modern signing. The glyph for "corn" is a poor match. The prehistoric icon is either a very graphic representation of the whole corn plant or a very abstract dot and grid glyph. The modern signing for corn is usually a mime of eating corn on the cob or, as shown in Chart 3, the gesture of scraping kernels off a cob. This is not a good match. But this is the exception and not the rule. When examining Chart 3, most of the icons and gestural representations are undeniable such as "death", "rainbow", "flight", "peace", "falling rain", etc., and they clearly demonstrate the unchanging nature of human beings and how they transmit ideas. We still think in very much the same way we did several hundred years ago. Some of the gestural representations when compared to the prehistoric icon could be debated such as "cloud" or "mountain", but if you keep in mind that the gesture is recreating the shape, form or movement of the thing being represented, and that the icon is attempting the same method to convey the idea, it is no wonder that there are so many similarities. This all simply means that sign language is a good place to look if you are trying to translate icons.

Another issue that will undoubtedly raise its semantically labored head will be that of "do these iconographic representations comprise a written language?" There, so far, is no evidence that these symbols represent any single "language", that is, a spoken form of communication. It is estimated that there were over two thousand distinct languages spoken across the Americas at the time of contact. Any human group with even limited mobility prehistorically in the Americas would need to be able to communicate with many other language groups. It is unlikely that the prehistoric traders learned dozens of languages; it is more tenable that they employed the single gestural language of signing. The fact that these symbols do not represent a single spoken language is the basis of the comparison between sign language gestures and the icons. These icons were probably used by several language groups, just as prehistoric signing was probably employed over large areas and by several distinct cultural clusters. Because these are primarily not phonetic representations allows the comparison. Sign language also does not necessarily employ sound. The absence of phonetic representation in the symbol combinations is the exact reason why the comparison to modern signing is possible. The ideas are being communicated, not the spoken words for the ideas. The ideas common to human behavior have not changed very much over the centuries. The way a bipedal, double fisted, frontal visioned, fire using omnivore relates the ideas also has not changed very much in a few hundred years.

Now that the analysis has been presented, the defense begins. I hardly expect academe to joyously accept the translations. I expect the opposite. Critics will attempt to shoot a thousand holes into the theory. Many of these holes may remain indefensible, but if one glyph in my analysis is correct, if one icon out of the several presented here is right, then for the first time in eight hundred years we can interpret previously unknown symbols into modern thought. I do not expect a thunderous ovation, I expect deafening criticism. Good. Sometimes you have to poke a hornet's nest to find the queen. The most important result of the publication of this theory will be that researchers will rethink petroglyphs, pictographs, kiva murals and ceramic decoration. That is my sole purpose. Look again, I think we may be missing something that is right in front of our noses. The forest of "hatchured 3mm. diagonal filler stylistic quadrants" may in fact be trees. A magnifying glass is not necessarily the best tool with which to examine an elephant.

A Word Concerning Mimbres Pottery

One pottery developmental sequence found in the Southwest prehistorically that at first seems to teem with icons are the Classic Mimbres Black-on-white pottery types, appearing around A.D. 1000 (Brody 1977, Cosgrove and Cosgrove 1932, Moulard 1984). These vessels abound with anthropomorphic and zoomorphic figures performing in a great variety of whimsical displays. These figures often represent a real physical human activity, such as gardening, weaving, or even pottery making (see figures 113, 114, and 115) (Moulard 1984). Other Mimbres vessels show half-human, half-animal figures interacting in a wide variety of prehistoric ceremonies; or animal figures behaving surprisingly realistically. (see figures 116 and 117). Mimbres pottery, in most cases where there are zoomorphic or anthropomorphic representations, seems to illustrate a known narrative. There are a multitude of common themes, cranes and decapitation, the warrior twins and their antics, representations of solar and lunar eclipses, and many stories the details of which are forever lost. Icons bleed in, but usually as a secondary element, painted in as an object being held or worn by the dramatic participants of the action or symbolically enumerated around or within an object or subject of the action. Mimbres pottery that illustrated zoomorphic or anthropomorphic action was not normally traded out of the Mimbres area (LeBlanc 1983). The majority of these vessels were used as mortuary offerings, and the themes depicted most likely reflect ceremonies or scenes associated with Mimbres life and possibly even the life of the deceased. Some Mimbres vessels were traded, however, the majority of these exhibited only geometric designs. Icons can be found on Mimbres pottery. These usually appear subtly utilized to clarify the meaning of the action being depicted. In general, Mimbres pottery does not seem to employ a great deal of iconography. Mimbres depictions demonstrate realism, at least to the Mimbrenos. They are similar to the illustrations found in children's books. The elements of the story being told, the actors and action, are incorporated into one representation. Some icons are present, however, they are not used as a primary communicative vehicle. White Mountain icon use differs from Mimbrenos icon use in that on the White Mountains examples, the iconography is the primary communicative vehicle. White Mountains examples will occasionally illustrate a known narrative, such as vessel SW1391a (see "The Smoking Gun"). When this occurs the result is virtually a Rosetta Stone of information because nearly all of the symbols used to create the narrative have unit meaning. In the case of Mimbres pottery the narrative is represented with more realistic detail, and symbols/icons are used as reenforcing elements.

Figure 113. Classic Mimbres vessel showing gardening. (From Moulard 1984)

Figure 114. Classic Mimbres Black-on-white showing weaver and a loom. (From Moulard 1984)

Figure 116. Classic Mimbres Black-on-white bowl showing half-human, half-zoomorph figure. (From Moulard 1984)

Figure 115. Classic Mimbres Black-on-white Bowl showing pottery painter and an attendant. (From Moulard 1984)

Figure 117. Classic Mimbres Black-on-white bowl. Coupling Antelope. (From Brody 1977)

Appendix I

Ceramic Representation of the Crab Nebula

At the University of Texas at Austin, Dr. Robert Robbins and Russell B. Westmoreland examined a sample of 800 Mimbres bowls from the Galaz site. By using representations of the rabbit found on many of these vessels as an indicator of lunar imagery, they then took a closer look at the bowls and counted all dots, projections, dashes, the number of feathers and anything else that could be counted. In all cases where the rabbit was found on the pottery, lunar numbers were also discovered, or the rabbit represented a lunar eclipse. The numbers 28, 29 or 30 days have all been used as the lunar phase period by the Indians of the western hemisphere, with "28 plus a day of invisibility" being most commonly found (Aveni 1980).

Eclipse symbolism on Mimbres vessels is represented by the rabbit, which embodies the moon, shown being eaten by a bird. It is a common Amerindian myth that an eclipse corresponds to something eating the sun or moon (Heizer 1974)

(see figures 118 and 119).

The most remarkable representation discovered during this research is a possible representation of the Crab Nebula explosion of Taurus. According to Japanese and Chinese observers, this phenomenon occurred in the early morning hours of July 5, 1054. Representations of this phenomenon in the prehistoric record of this continent have so far eluded research. After the explosion, the star was visible during daylight hours for 23 days. The Mimbres depiction (see figure 120) shows the lunar rabbit with another body in the sky. This second representation with the rabbit has 23 points radiating from the center, which could portray the 23 days when the star was visible during daylight. The bowl shown in figure 118 has been dated using other associated cultural material discovered in the room where it was found. The dates that were obtained are consistent with the temporal occurrence of the exploding star.

Figure 118. Mimbres bowl showing a rabbit being eaten by a bird. These depictions could represent a lunar eclipse. (From Robbins 1991)

Figure 119. Mimbres bowl with a bird eating a rabbit possibly representing the lunar eclipse. (From Robbins 1991)

Figure 120. Mimbres bowl showing the lunar rabbit with another body in the sky with 23 rays, possibly the Crab Nebula explosion of A.D. 1054 (From Robbins 1991)

Appendix II

Doorway/Passageway/Emergence

During the 1992 field excavation season at Raven Site Ruin a painted stone tablet was unearthed from room 27 in the South Pueblo (see photo 97). The tablet was wonderfully preserved with blue, black, yellow, red and white paints depicting the emergence from one level of existence to another, or possibly migration of a clan group from one area or pueblo to another. There are five icons displayed on the tablet, four of which have known meanings, and one which can now be translated for the first time. At the top of the tablet, there is a rainbow above two rain clouds. The rain clouds are complete with a "flight" icon on top of the terracing of each cloud, and four columns of rain below each. The use of the number four in pueblo mythology is abundant, and probably stems from the belief that this world is the fourth world of emergence. These rain clouds are beautifully graphic depictions and they are very similar to the rain cloud examples found on Zuni kachinas. This could indicate that the stone tablet was made quite late in prehistory. Other cultural material excavated in room 27 that can be dated, including ceramic types, indicates that the room was occupied between A.D. 1400 and A.D. 1500. The rain clouds and rainbow are contained in an arched field of turquoise blue at the top of the stone tablet. Below this colored field are two icons: a "zigzag" depicting movement or migration and a "T" shaped glyph which can now be translated to mean "doorway/passageway/emergence".

This symbolic "T" shaped glyph can be found throughout the prehistoric Southwest, most notably as the shape of many of the doorways at Chaco Canyon. There has been a great debate in the past concerning the "T" shaped doors. One theory claims that the doors were shaped this way to accommodate entrance to the room while wearing a backpack. Another theory speculates that the doors were shaped this way so an enemy would have to bend over when entering and this would slow the attack and accommodate defense of the pueblo.

Another theory speculates that the small area at the bottom of the door allows air into the central fire box, assuming of course, that the rest of the doorway was covered by a skin or weaving. The architecture at Chaco is dramatic, spectacular, an expressive exaltation of humankind's ability. It is not pragmatic, nor are the doorways. These "T" shaped doorways are symbolic representations of "emergence or passageway" as is the glyph found on the stone tablet from room 27 at Raven Site.

Another common "T" shaped cultural object with the same meaning can be seen when examining the stone hatch covers which guard the entrances of the kivas at Raven Site. These carved lithic covers are humorously referred to as "toilet seats" because of their curious shape (see photo 98). It is not the stone cover itself which displays the "T" shaped "emergence/passageway" idea, but instead the central negative space created by the carved stone. This "T" shaped glyph may have evolved from the sipapu, the symbolic entrance from the world below to this world above. This unusual hatch cover shape could be an extension of the idea of the sipapu opening, i.e. the passageway or emergence from one realm to another.

This "T" shaped symbol has also been found on jewelry inlays at Raven Site. The shape is so unique that its symbolic meaning probably survives even in this form (see photo 99).

A very convincing artifact with the "T" shaped "emergence/passageway" glyph can be seen on two stone objects as seen in photo 100. These are models of prehistoric pueblo rooms, three stories high. The "T" shaped doorways can be seen on the front of the models. One of these wonderful artifacts was excavated at Raven Site from the floor of room 7, along with several other carved sandstone objects including several sandstone bowls, an incense burner and a small unused ax. These stone objects still retain red and yellow paint on the exterior. The larger of the two pueblo models was

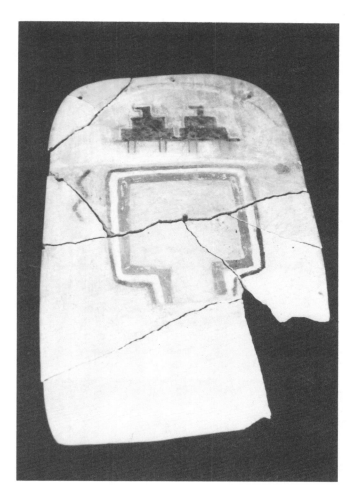

Photo 97. Stone tablet excavated from room 27, Raven Site Ruin. The central "T" shaped glyph indicates "doorway/passageway/migration" and the fact that it was painted yellow may be an indication of the direction of movement. The small "zigzag" to the left of the "T" shaped glyph indicates movement.

Photo 98. Stone hatch covers found guarding the entranceways to the kivas at Raven Site. The negative space created by the carved stone serendipitously forms the "T" shaped "passageway/emergence" glyph. These probably are reminiscent of the sipapu openings on the kiva floors.

discovered by a rancher in the area of Raven Site while plowing his field. Also discovered at the sametime was a large cloud blower sandstone pipe also with yellow and red paint still present on the exterior. The symbolic "T" shaped doorways on these artifacts enabled researchers to identify the objects as pueblo models.

What is undoubtedly significant is the red and yellow paint on the sandstone objects found in association with the pueblo models, and the fact that both individual groups of artifacts contain one object that is capable of producing smoke i.e. the pipe and the incense burner.

That colors are associated with direction is pueblo culture. Red indicates the direction south and yellow north. The painted slab discovered in room 27 at Raven Site Ruin (see photo 97) depicts the "T" shaped "door/emergence/passageway" glyph primarily in yellow paint, which may indicate a direction of movement or migration. The slab could be a directional marker, indicating the direction of the last migration from Raven Site to the north. Ceramics from Raven Site indicate that at least one major clan migrated north to Second Mesa after A.D. 1450 (See the translation of vessel SW1509). The modern Hopi claim that the prehistoric pueblo people left indicators as to the direction of their migrations. This stone slab and its glyph may be indicating the direction of the last migration from Raven Site to the north.

At the very least, this remarkable artifact demonstrates an association between the "T" shaped glyph and the red and yellow pigments with which the glyph is created. The two pueblo models mentioned above and illustrated in photo 100 also demonstrate this connection between the colors and the glyph.

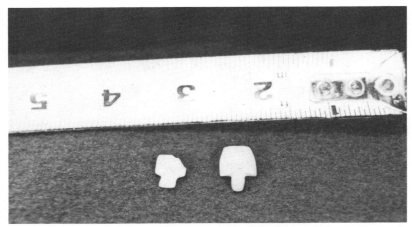

Photo 99. Jewelry inlay with the "T" shaped "emergence/passageway" glyph.

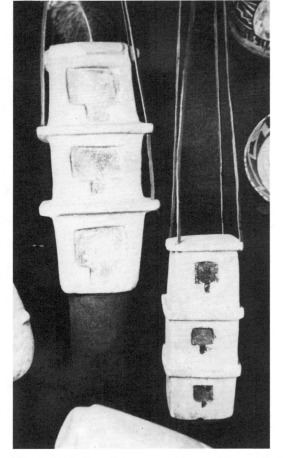

Photo 100. Sandstone pueblo models with the "T" shaped doorways. Each model is surrounded by its associated objects. These objects exhibit red and yellow paint as does the stone tablet in photo 97. These colors may be directional indicators.

The "T" glyph, i.e. "Doorway, Passageway, Emergence" and the ceramic "Spirit Break".

Now that several examples of the "T" shaped glyph have been presented, I would like to offer a comparison between the "T" glyph and a very common ceramic design. Found throughout the ceramic assemblage of the Southwest is a design element known as the "spirit break". This consists of a band which encircles the vessel, usually around the neck of ollas or the interior of bowls. This band has a single break, or gap. This break or gap in the band is known as the "spirit break" of the vessel. It allows the spirit of the vessel to escape without the necessity of actually smashing the piece. This "spirit break" is called the "onane" by the Zuni. It is a road to life, a way to *emerge* from the sipapu (see photos 101, 102 and 103).

The "spirit break" can still be found today on many of the modern ceramics being produced by Native Americans and occasionally on Navajo weavings.

Throughout prehistory, ritual "killing" of ceramics and other artifacts has been performed, often associated with the burial of the artifact with the dead. In many cases this ritual killing was achieved by the total destruction of the artifact and the remaining pieces being interred with the dead. This ritual "killing" of the ceramic vessel is not entirely limited to grave offerings. Cushing (1800) observed a ceremony during his stay with the Zuni in the nineteenth century where the Katsina clowns went from house to house and smashed vessels of the finest quality. These vessels were purposely left outside near the rooftop doorways to accommodate the clowns. Many of the highest quality White Mountain Redwares that are found at Raven Site are splattered over a wide provenance of the site. This may be explained by a similar prehistoric ceremony as was observed by Cushing.

Many groups chose to remove only a small piece or area of the object before burying it with their deceased. The most notable examples are the "kill holes" found on the center bottom of Mimbres bowls. The bowl is placed over the face of the deceased, and the bottom of the bowl is punched out to allow the spirit of the vessel to escape. This leaves the bowl basically intact (see photo 104).

Other examples of the ritual "killing" of ceramics is to break off a small area of the rim of the bowl or jar before it is placed in the grave with the deceased. Photo 105 shows three small Gila Polychrome bowls that are similarly rim mutilated.

Grinding or notching the edge of the bowl is another form of "killing" the vessel.

All of the above examples express the same rational. The spirit of the vessel must *emerge*, be

Photo 101. "Spirit break" encircling the neck of an olla.

able to leave/move/travel/escape, i.e. pass from one place to another. The smashing of the vessel accommodates this need, as does rim mutilation, as does the "spirit break" painted on the rim or neck of the ceramics.

The "T" shaped glyph represents emergence/migration/doorway/passageway/movement from one place to another. If you examine the form of the "spirit break" as it is represented on ceramics, it is not difficult to see the similarity between the negative space created by the total glyph, and the central negative space created by the "T" glyph. They are identical except that the "T" glyph has more right angled attributes. These right angled attributes are undoubtedly due only to the fact that it is a more difficult construction job to build rounded corners out of stone in the case of doorways.

Examine photo 98, the stone hatch covers which guard the kiva entrances and the examples of ceramic "spirit breaks" presented in photos 101, 102, 103. The similarity of form is obvious.

What do you do when you go through a doorway? You pass from one realm to another, you move, you emerge. The painted ceramic "spirit breaks" create a doorway for the spirit of the vessel to move from the realm of this world to the next level of existence in pueblo thought.

Those mysterious "T" shaped doorways that are found so abundantly throughout the architecture of the Southwest are not pragmatic. They are not built to slow down an enemy, vent a room, or accommodate a backpack. They *are* a symbol. They allow the spirits to freely enter and exit the dwelling.

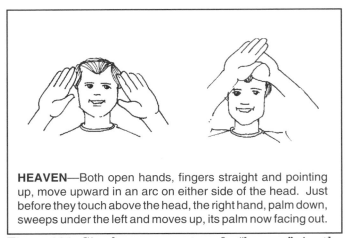

HEAVEN—Both open hands, fingers straight and pointing up, move upward in an arc on either side of the head. Just before they touch above the head, the right hand, palm down, sweeps under the left and moves up, its palm now facing out.

Figure 121. Sign language gesture for "heaven", i.e. the passing from this realm to the next.

Photo 102. "Spirit break" with "cloud" attributes.

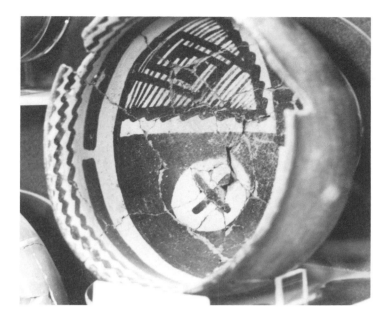

Photo 103. "Spirit break" encircling the edge of a Gila Polychrome bowl.

Photo 104. Mimbres bowl with "kill hole"

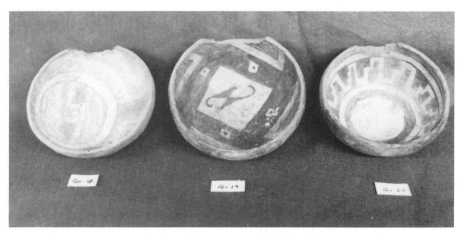

Photo 105. Three small Gila Polychrome bowls with rim mutilation.

Appendix 3

Ceramic Types and Dates

Throughout this text there are references to various ceramic "types" and their associated dates. It is usually not possible to directly date a ceramic vessel, unless there is sufficient food residue within the vessel, under the rim, etc, to provide a C14 date. Rooms in prehistoric pueblos are excavated, ceramics of a particular type are discovered in the room, and the room is dated from charcoal or a wood beam sample or some other dating method. For example, Tularosa Black-on-white jars are always found with material that dates between A.D. 1200-1300

It is fairly safe to say that this ceramic style was produced within that 100 year period. By simply recognizing Tularosa as a ceramic "type" it is then possible to postulate that other materials in other rooms were made during the production of Tularosa ceramics, i.e. A.D. 1200-1300. The following is a very rudimentary list of the major ceramic types illustrated in this book. They are listed in temporal sequences, and organized by their spacial distribution. The dates of their production are also listed.

White Mountain Redwares

This ceramic tradition consists of a sequence of ceramic types which includes black on red vessels and Polychromes, i.e. vessels with black on red and the addition later of white kaolin paint, originally on the exterior of bowls and later on the interior and exterior. The red base color is the slip, a thin creamy colored clay which is rubbed into the surfaces of the vessel with a polishing stone.

Puerco Black-on-red .... **A.D. 1000-1200**

This ceramic type is the first of the White Mountain Redwares. Slipped red on the interior and exterior of bowls and the exterior of jars. Paint can be a faded brown or good black and it penetrates the slip. Temper is ground sherd or quartz sand. Bowl exteriors are never decorated. The interior center bottom of bowls is usually not decorated, but left as an open field, often circular.

There are no examples of Puerco Black and Red vessels illustrated in this text because the use of iconography on this ceramic type has so far not been observed by this author, with the exception of one Kokopelli glyph (Carlson 1970: 12 figure b).

Wingate Black-on-red .... **A.D. 1050-1200**

Slipped red on the interior and exterior of bowls and on the exterior of jars. Sherd temper. Decoration goes to the rim and may cover the whole interior of the bowl or leave the center bottom undecorated. There is a marked

increase in the use of interlocked solid and hatchured units.

There are no examples of Wingate Black on Red in this text, because no definite iconography has been observed. The scrolls and interlocked units resemble "wind" and "earth/land" and "four directions" in some cases, but better examples are found later in this ceramic developmental sequence.

Wingate Polychrome .... **A.D. 1125-1200**

Same as Wingate Black on Red except that the slip is sometimes orange and the exterior of bowls is decorated in wide designs of white kaolin paint. The addition of this white paint defines this ceramic type as the first White Mountain Redware Polychrome. The exterior of bowls are slipped in white, and then the red is added over the white slip.

No examples are presented in the text, although symbols do begin to appear on the exterior of bowls, usually in the form of handprints executed in the white paint.

St. Johns Black-on-red .... **A.D. 1175-1300**

Vessels are slipped red or orange red and have a sherd temper. Designs are interlocked solid and hatchured units, scrolls and frets are common.

This type seldom displays iconography and no examples are presented in the text.

St. Johns Polychrome .... A.D. 1175-1300

Slipped red or orange on the interior and exterior of bowls and on the exterior of jars. Sherd temper. Design elements are the same as St. Johns Black on Red. The exterior of bowls displays white kaolin paint similar to Wingate Polychrome, except that the white design elements are narrower, more linear, and the exterior is first slipped in red rather than white. The white paint is applied over the red slip.

The exterior of bowls often displays iconography in the form of handprints, centipedes and other life forms. Vessel SW1008 (photos 10 and 67), "Determined Man", is an under-fired St. Johns Polychrome.

Springerville Polychrome .......A.D. 1250-1300

Springerville Polychrome is differentiated from St. Johns Polychrome by the addition of black lines on the exterior of bowls along with the white kaolin designs.

Pinedale Polychrome.................A.D. 1275-1325

Slipped red or orange on the interior and exterior of bowls and on the exterior of jars. Sherd temper. Design elements are similar to St. Johns Polychromes with the exception of unit elements of design on the exterior of bowls. These unit elements are often butterflies, serpents, birds and crosses. Both black and white paint is used in the execution of these designs.

Figure 64 is an example of an exterior serpent design on a Pinedale Polychrome.

Pinedale Black-on-red ...............A.D. 1275-1325

Same as Pinedale Polychrome but without the addition of white kaolin paint.

Cedar Creek Polychrome.........A.D. 1300-1375

Slipped red or orange on the interiors and exteriors of bowls and on the exterior of jars. Jars sometimes have a white slip on the neck or shoulders. The exterior of bowls display design elements that are similar to Pinedale Polychromes, i.e. individual units that are often recognizable as symbols, but Cedar Creek Polychromes begin to link these units into a very linear band, often including a black band totally around the exterior rim of the bowl. Photo 52 is a Cedar Creek Polychrome sherd

showing the "four directions" glyph.

Fourmile Polychrome ................A.D. 1325-1400

Slipped red or orange on the interior and exterior of bowls and on the exterior of jars. Jars often have a white slip on the neck and shoulders. A black banding on the rim of bowls both on the interior and exterior which defines a field of design is diagnostic of the type. This exterior band often includes a second black band several centimeters below the top band. The area between is filled with design elements. Designs of both black and white are found on the interior and exterior.

Examples in the text include: SW1391a (cover photo)(photos 11, 20, 31, 35, 47, 75, 89). SW1013 (photos 2, 8, 84, 88, 90, 94). SW1012 (photos 3, 78). Pi2 (photos 4, 13, 22, 41, 48). SW305 (photo 16, 32). and SW1011 (photos 17, 21, 36, 65). The Fourmile Polychromes exhibit abundant iconography.

Show Low Polychrome ...........A.D. 1325-1400

Virtually identical to Fourmile Polychromes. Fourmile Polychrome jars are often typed as Show Low Polychromes because of the white slip on the neck and shoulders.

Point of Pines Polychrome ....A.D. 1400-1450

Point of Pines Polychromes are late copies of Fourmile Polychromes. They were produced by a group of people who probably did not previously make painted pottery. The execution of designs is poor, lacking the quality of the Fourmile vessels.

An example of this type in the text is vessel SW1501 (photos 12, 23, and 73).

There are several Black-on-white ceramic types which are found in association with the above Redware ceramics. The two that are primarily relevant to this research are Reserve Black-on-white and Tularosa Black-on-white.

Reserve Black-on-white ..........A.D. 1000-1100

Paste is grey to white and the interior of bowls is slipped white and decorated with black paint. Designs are simple, very geometric, and well executed. Fired in a reducing atmosphere.

Examples include: vessel C1-1 (photos 58 and 72), and figures 35, 37 and 68.

Tularosa Black-on-white .... A.D. 1200-1300
Paste is grey to white. Bowls and dippers are slipped white on the interior and exterior, jars on the exterior. Fired in a reducing atmosphere. Black paint can be vibrant or dull, occasionally on an area of the vessel the black will have a brown or even reddish tinge. This is due to oxygen exposure during firing. Designs incorporate an abundance of interlocked units, one hatchured and one solid. Scrolls and terraces are common. Most of the ollas found at Raven Site are of the Tularosa type. Many of these exhibit an areola around the neck of the jar.

Examples in the text include: Sherd, room 17 (photos 6 and 54.) SW1003, (photos 18, 19, 38, 43, 45, 50, 55, 66, 69, 70, 76, 82 and 85). SW1495a (photo 46 and figure 77). Sherd, room 18 (photo 92.)

A second ceramic tradition evolved at Raven Site Ruin and continued beyond the White Mountain Redware ceramic sequence. The Zuni glazewares appeared. These vessels use a lead glaze that fires to a glassy or vitreous appearance. Around the year A.D. 1300 there was a split in the ceramic developments. One tradition continued to use the non-lead paints which produced clean, controlled design elements. The other ceramic tradition began to use the lead glazes. These lead glazes run when fired, which often produced blurred and "sloppy" looking designs. All of the following types are found at Raven Site, with the exception of Matsaki Polychrome, the very last in the sequence.

Heshotauthla Polychrome ...... A.D. 1275-1300

Heshotauthla Black-on-red ..... A.D. 1275-1300

Kwakina Polychrome .... A.D. 1325-1400
Examples of Kwakina Polychrome in the text include: figure 48 and vessel SW1383a (photo 26).

Pinnawa Glaze-on-white .. A.D. 1350-1450
Examples include: SW1494 (photo 24). SW1390a (photo 25). SW1028 (photo 91).

Pinnawa Red-on-white ..... A.D. 1350-1450

Kechipawan Polychrome A.D. 1375-1475

Red-on-buff (unnamed) .... A.D. 1450 +
The Unnamed Red on Buff shown in the text is vessel SW1509 (photos 14, 26a, 26b, 26c, 26d, 56 and 59).

Matsaki Polychrome .... A.D. 1475-1680

The following ceramic types are found at Raven Site, but were not made there. They were made south of Raven Site below the Mogollon Rim and traded.

Pinto Polychrome .... A.D. 1265 +

Gila Polychrome .... A.D. 1300 +
Examples in the text include: Pi5 (photos 5, 9, and 80). Vessel 1330b (photos 27 and 40). Vessel Qr83 (photos 86 and 96).

Tonto Polychrome .... A.D. 1300 +
Examples in the text include: SW1508 (photos 30, 87, and 95) and QrPi21 (photos 29 and 60).

Mortars and pestles used to grind sherds into temper and colored minerals into pigments. Examples 2 and 9 still retain the ground turquoise pigment on the surface. Example 7 was used to grind iron ore into red slip pigment. Example 6 was used to grind the yellow pigment limonite and the small dish (Example 10) still contains the ground limonite powder.

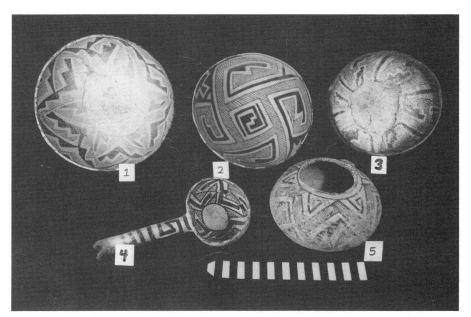

Reserve Black-on-white. Designs are simple, hachuring usually contrasts the element which it fills, but not always. Line work is very well executed but not as fine as later Cibola White Wares. Examples 1 and 3 show heavy wear. The dipper is a late Reserve Black-on-white, showing similarities to Tularosa Black-on-white. The jar shown in Example 5 demonstrates very heavy wear, the neck is completely worn away. This jar could be typed as Snowflake Black-on-white.

Glossary

A.D.: Latin, *anno Domini,* in the year of the Lord. Used to designate time, for example, "A.D. 1200 " means that the event occurred in the twelve-hundredth year of the Christian era. B.C. dates count backwards. Therefore, "1200 B.C." would refer to a time occurring 1200 years prior to the Christian era.

Anasazi: A Navajo word meaning "alien ancient one" sometimes interpreted to mean "ancient enemy". Basketmaker/pueblo culture of the plateau area of northern Arizona, New Mexico, Utah and Colorado. Contemporaneous with the Mogollon and Hohokam culture areas to the south and west.

Ahaiyuta: Zuni war twin, brother of Matsailema. According to Zuni legend, these brothers killed the monster Atahsaia, beheaded and disemboweled him and flung the head into the heavens where it became the lying star. The entrails became the Milky Way.

Amerindian: Any Native American Indian cultural group that inhabits or has inhabited the Americas, North or South.

Anthropomorphic: Anthropo refers to "man" and morphic "change". This term refers to any representation that resembles the human form. The term zoomorphic is any representation that resembles an animal.

Apache: From the Zuni word "apachu" or "enemy". Group of tribes forming the most southern group of the Athapaskan speakers.

Archaeoastronomy: Research area of archaeology that examines prehistoric correlations with astronomy or celestial events.

Areola: Small border or defined area. In ceramic analysis the areola refers to the border around the neck of a jar or olla. Tularosa ollas dating A.D. 1200-1300 often have a raised area around the neck of the olla; this raised areola is diagnostic of the pottery type.

Atahsaia: Zuni monster of legend that was beheaded and disemboweled by the warrior twins. His head and entrails were thrown into the sky. The head became the lying star, the entrails the Milky Way.

Athapaskan: Native American Indian group, speakers of the Athapaskan language which consists of three major dialectic areas. This language group includes the Navajo and Apache. The Athapaskans arrived quite late into the Southwest, after A.D. 1500.

B.C.: See A.D.

Casas Grandes: Large prehistoric trade center located in the Chihuahuan area of Mexico. Occupied as early as A.D. 1060 and lasting until about A.D. 1340 . This pueblo produced a variety of trade items including lost wax cast copper bells and live parrots.

Cedar Creek: A White Mountain Redware ceramic type. Polychrome, using red slip, and black and white interior and exterior paints. Produced from A.D. 1300-1375.

Ceramic Types: A style of pottery, usually designated as a type based on color, form, temper and spacial and temporal distribution.

Crab Nebula: A star that exploded in the Taurus system in the year A.D. 1054. The star was visible in the daylight sky for 23 days. This was recorded by Chinese astronomers and a possible depiction appears on Mimbres pottery (see appendix I).

Cuneiform: Prehistoric Mesopotamian written language which used a reed stylus and wet clay tablet. Invented by the Sumerians about 3200 B.C.

Cultural Areas: Regional distribution of a particular set of cultural traits, i.e. specific ceramics, architecture, stone tools, language, etc. that are unique to one group of people. The three main cultural areas found in the prehistoric Southwest are the Anasazi, Mogollon and Hohokam.

Dating Techniques: Various methods used to establish/assign a calendar date to an artifact or event prehistorically. These methods include stratigraphy, carbon 14, dendrochronology, pollen analysis, ceramic typology, potassium/argon, obsidian hydration, desert varnish measurement and archaeomagnetic measurements.

Dendrochronology: Tree ring dating technique developed by astronomer A. E. Douglass, used primarily in the Southwest. The widths of tree rings vary depending upon the growth cycles, wet years, dry years and other conditions. By tracking the growth rings from the present into the past, a sequence of ring widths has been established. By comparing a prehistoric wood or charcoal sample with an unknown date to this sequence it is often possible to determine what year the tree was cut.

Desert Varnish: A naturally occurring discoloration on rocks of the Southwest. Produced on the surface of the stone over long periods of time due to oxidation, moisture, seepage and the natural minerals in the rock. It is this varnish that was pecked or chiseled away to produce petroglyphs. There have been recent attempts to date petroglyphs by measuring desert varnish layers.

Determinatives: also "key signs". In the evolution of written languages, determinatives or key signs appear, usually without a spoken value, but indicating important information. Determinatives are used in a variety of ways. On the vessels presented in this study, determinatives are used to indicate emphasis and to indicate which glyphs are to be read together.

Emblem: A visible sign of an idea. An object, or figure of an object, symbolizing another object or idea by natural aptness or association.

Ethnology: Science that deals with man, his origins, distributions, relations, and with the peculiarities that characterized different groups. The comparative and analytical study of cultures.

Fire Clouding: An isolated field of discoloration found on the surface of prehistoric ceramics caused by firing.

Fourmile: A White Mountain Redware ceramic type, dating A.D. 1325-1400. A Polychrome, this type exhibits the height of iconography use in the White Mountains. Bowls and jars are slipped red on the interior and exterior and black and white paint are used on both surfaces.

Gila: Ceramic type produced primarily below the Mogollon Rim in Arizona, dating A.D. 1300+. Examples in this study are Polychromes, with red slipped exteriors and black and white interiors in the case of bowls.

Heshotauthla: A Zuni glazeware Polychrome pottery found in the White Mountains of Arizona. Vessels are slipped red on the interior and exterior, black paint is vitreous, white is chalky and kaolin. This type dates from A.D. 1275-1300.

Museum at White Mountain Archaeological Center.

Hieroglyphs: A picture script of the ancient Egyptian priesthood. It is believed that hieroglyphs became a flowing realistic/graphic form of writing aided by the medium of papyrus.

Hohokam: Prehistoric cultural group who arrived in the Southwest from Mexico and occupied the areas around Phoenix, Arizona and as far north as Flagstaff. Contemporaneous with the Anasazi and Mogollon cultural groups. Hohokam culture exhibits many unique traits such as paddle and anvil ceramic construction, the use of ball courts, extensive irrigation and unusual lithic material such as paint pallets.

Hopi: A pueblo people of northeastern Arizona. Possible descendants of the prehistoric pueblo groups. A very esoteric society with practicing Kachina cults.

Hukangwaa: A Hopi storm god who assisted the war twins after a smoking test.

Icon: Illustrations of a subject by pictures or other representations. A recognized unit.

Janus Face: An anthropomorphic representation found on both Mimbres and Casas Grandes ceramics which depicts the human face with gnashing teeth and a triangular fleshless nose. Possibly a "death" symbol.

Kaolin: A white chalky paint found on prehistoric ceramics, especially the White Mountain Redwares.

Katsina (Kachina): An ancestral spirit of the pueblo peoples believed to visit the pueblos at seasonal ceremonies, and/or doll representing such a spirit.

Key Signs: See "Determinatives".

Kiva: A ceremonial chamber. Kivas come in all shapes and sizes including round, rectangular, square and D shaped. Entrance and lighting usually from the roof, usually includes an altar, hearth and sipapu.

Kokopelli: The humpbacked flute player. Depictions are found abundantly on the rock art of the Southwest and occasionally on ceramics. The exact nature of this deity is unknown. The humpback often resembles a backpack full of seeds. Kokopelli often proudly exhibits an erection.

Kwakina: A ceramic type. Zuni glazeware. Bowls are slipped red outside and white inside. Black glaze paint inside and white and black outside. Produced between A.D. 1325-1400.

Matsailema: One of the Zuni war twins.

Mogollon: Prehistoric cultural group contemporaneous with the Anasazi and Hohokam. Located in south/central Arizona and New Mexico.

Mimbres: Prehistoric cultural subgroup of the Mogollon, located in southwestern New Mexico. Most noted for black and white bowls exhibiting graphic anthropomorphic and zoomorphic depictions. These vessels were primarily used as mortuary offerings.

Morpheme: A meaningful linguistic unit that contains no smaller meaningful parts.

Nadir: Zuni directional indicator. Downward, opposite of zenith.

Navajo: An Athapaskan people of northern Arizona and New Mexico and ranging into Colorado and Utah. The Navajo arrived late into the Southwest, approximately A.D. 1500.

Ne'wekwe: Zuni clown society. When these clowns appear in public they are striped with black and white paint. They are associated with the night sky, winter and the underworld.

Omauwu: Hopi "rain cloud"

Onane: Spirit break. A gap left in the design of a vessel or weaving which allows the spirit of the piece to escape.

Olla: A large ceramic jar.

Palunhoya: One of the Hopi war twins.

Patki: Second Hopi phratral organization, "cloud/house".

Petroglyph: A prehistoric symbol representation pecked or chiseled into stone.

Pictograph: A prehistoric symbol representation usually executed on stone. These representations are painted, not pecked or chiseled.

Pinto: Ceramic type found primarily below the Mogollon Rim in Arizona. Bowl exteriors are slipped red and the interiors are slipped white and then painted in black. This ceramic type is the forerunner of both Gila and Tonto Polychromes.

Pochteca: Prehistoric traders. These wanderers traveled across the Southwest trading turquoise, copper bells and even live parrots.

Polychrome: More than two colors. Ceramic analysis includes the background or slip color of the vessel. If a vessel has an overall red slip and is then painted in black and white, it is considered a Polychrome.

Protohistorically: History, as we refer to the term, begins with written records. In the Southwest, this period begins around A.D. 1540 with Spanish contact. Anything before Spanish contact is prehistoric and anything after Spanish contact is historic. Protohistoric refers to the grey area in between the two temporal designations.

Provenience: The location of an artifact.

Puukonhoya: One of the Hopi war twins.

Rain Streamer: A symbol for rain, rainbow or rain bringing, found protruding from the rear of zoomorphic representations.

Rock Art: A term which refers to any prehistoric representation depicted on stone, be it a painted pictograph or a pecked/chiseled petroglyph.

Rosetta Stone: A stone tablet found in 1799 that provided the first clue to deciphering Egyptian hieroglyphs. The tablet displayed the same story written in three different languages.

Salado: Prehistoric culture in Arizona with a merging of Mogollon and Anasazi traits from A.D. 1100-1450.

Sherd: A fragment of pottery.

Sikyatki: A prehistoric pueblo of the "firewood" people of the Hopi. Located at Walpi mesa in northeastern Arizona.

Sipapu: Passageway to the underworld in pueblo thought.

Slip: A thick soupy clay paste, sometimes colored, that is applied to a ceramic vessel before the paint is applied. The slip is rubbed into the surface of the vessel using a polishing stone. It then becomes the background color for that area (interior/exterior) of the vessel.

Talawipiki: Hopi "lightning".

Tanaka: Hopi "rainbow"

Temper: Coarse material added to clays to prevent cracking when fired. Common tempers are sand, ground pottery sherds and shell.

Tradition: Referring to ceramic typology this simply means a group of ceramics that share common elements, such as provenience, style and most notably a developmental sequence.

Umtak-ina: Hopi god, "the thunder".

Vitreous: Glass-like. After A.D. 1300 lead glazes were introduced in the White Mountains. These produced a shiny glaze with good color, but the glazing tended to run during firing. This limited the controlled designs of earlier times and may have hampered the continued use of meaningful symbolism on ceramics.

White Mountain Redwares: A ceramic tradition found in the White Mountains of Arizona, beginning with the Puerco Black-on-red ceramics around A.D. 1000 and continuing through the Fourmile and Point of Pines Polychromes to around A.D. 1450.

Yoki: Hopi "rain".

Zenith: Zuni and Hopi directional indicator. The point above, opposite of nadir or below.

Zoomorphic: A representation that resembles an animal or has animal attributes.

Zuni: Pueblo people of Arizona and New Mexico. Possible descendants of the prehistoric pueblo peoples. Practicing Katsina cults.

Bibliography

Anderson, Keith
1971 *Excavations at Betatakin and Keet Seel. The Kiva* 37;1-29.

Antonsen, Elmer H.
1989 *The Runes: The Earliest Germanic Writing System. The Origins of Writing.* University of Nebraska Press 137-159. Lincoln, Nebraska

Aveni, A.F.
1980 *Skywatchers of Ancient Mexico.* University of Texas Press. Austin, Texas.

Barnes, F.A.
1982 *Canyon Country Prehistoric Rock Art.* Wasatch Publishers Inc. Salt Lake City, Utah.

Barnett, Franklin
1973 *Dictionary of Prehistoric Indian Artifacts of the American Southwest.* Northland Press. Flagstaff, Arizona.

Barry, John
1981 *American Indian Pottery.* Books Americana. Florence, Alabama.

Bellamy, James A.
1989 *The Arabic Alphabet. The Origins of Writing.* University of Nebraska Press 91-103. Lincoln, Nebraska.

Boas, Franz
1927 *Primitive Art.* H. Aschehoug and Co., Oslo. Oslo Institute for Comparative Research in Human Culture. Oslo, Norway.

Brew, J. O.
1943 *On the Pueblo IV and on the Kachina*, Tlaloc Relations. In *El Norte de Mexico y el Sur de los Estados Unidos*, Tercera. *Reunion de Mesa Redonda sobre Problemas Antropologicas de Mexico y Centro America.* Sociedad Mexicana de Antropologia. Mexico City, Mexico.

Brody, J.J.
1977 *Mimbres Painted Pottery.* School of American Research, Santa Fe. University of New Mexico Press. Albuquerque, New Mexico.

1983 *Mimbres Pottery. Ancient Art of the American Southwest.* Hudson Hills Press, New York, New York

Brose, David S., J. A. Brown, and D. W. Penney
1985 *Ancient Art of the American Woodland Indians.* Harry N. Abrams, Inc. New York, New York.

Bunzel, Ruth L.
1932 *Zuni Kachinas: An Analytical Study.* Forty-seventh Annual Report of the Bureau of American Ethnology, 1929-30. Washington D.C.

Butterworth, R. R. and M. Flodin
1983 *The Perigee Visual Dictionary of Signing.* Putnam Publishing Group. New York, New York.

Carlson, Roy L.
1970 *White Mountain Redware. A Pottery Tradition of East-Central Arizona and Western New Mexico.* Anthropological Papers of the University of Arizona. Number 19. The University of Arizona Press. Tucson, Arizona.

Carr, Pat
1979 *Mimbres Mythology.* University of Texas, Southwestern Studies, Monograph No. 56. El Paso, Texas

Cordell, Linda S.
1984 *Prehistory of the Southwest.* Department of Anthropology, University of New Mexico, Albuquerque, New Mexico. Academic Press, Inc. New York, New York.

Cosgrove, H. S. and C. B. Cosgrove
1932 *The Swarts Ruin: A Typical Mimbres Site in Southwestern New Mexico.* Papers of the Peabody Museum of Archaeology and Ethnology, vol. 15, no. 1. Cambridge, Massachusetts.

Costello, Elaine.
1983 *Signing, How to Speak With Your Hands.* 6th edition. Bantam Books. New York, New York.

Cross, Frank Moore
1989 *The Invention and Development of the Alphabet. The Origins of Writing.* University of Nebraska Press 77-91. Lincoln, Nebraska.

Cushing, Frank H.
1882-83 *A Study of Pueblo Pottery as Illustrative of Zuni Culture Growth.* Fourth Annual Report of the Bureau of American Ethnology. Washington, D.C.

1880-81 *Zuni Fetishes.* Second Annual Report of the Bureau of American Ethnology. Washington, D.C.

1979 *Zuni.* University of Arizona Press. Tucson, Arizona.

1979 *Zuni Folk Tales.* University of Arizona Press. Tucson, Arizona.

Dean, Jeffrey S.
1970 *Aspects of Tsegi phase social organization: a trial reconstruction. In Reconstruction Prehistoric Pueblo Societies*, edited by William A. Longacre, pp. 140-174. School of American Research, Santa Fe, and the University of New Mexico Press, Albuquerque, New Mexico.

Dedera, Don
1975 *Navajo Rugs.* The Northland Press, Flagstaff, AZ

Durkheim, Imile and Marcel Mauss
1963   *Primitive Classification.*   University of Chicago Press. Chicago, Illinois

Ellis, Florence Hawley and Hammack Laurens
1968   *The Inner Sanctum of Feather Cave, A Mogollon Sun and Earth Shrine Linking Mexico and the Southwest.* American Antiquity 33:25-44.

Fewkes, Jesse Walter
1895-96*Sikyatki and Its Pottery.* Excerpt (pp. 631-728) Archeological Expedition to Arizona in 1895. Seventeenth Annual Report of the Bureau of American Ethnology to the Secretary of the Smithsonian Institution, 1895-96. Washington, D.C.

1895   *Designs on Prehistoric Hopi Pottery.* Dover Publications Inc., New York, New York.

Fisher, Henry George
1989   *The Origin of Egyptian Hieroglyphs. The Origins of Writing,* University of Nebraska Press 59-77. Lincoln, Nebraska.

Forde, C. D.
1931   *Hopi Agriculture and Land Ownership,* Royal Anthropological Institute 61: 357-405.

Furst, Peter T.
1974a *Ethnographic Analogy in the Interpretation of West Mexican Art.* In *The Archaeology of West Mexico.* ed. Betty Bell (Ajijie, Jalisco; West Mexican Society for Advanced Study).

Grant, Campbell
1981   *Rock Art of the American Indian.* Outbooks, Golden, Colorado.

Green, M. W.
1989   *Early Cuneiform. The Origins of Writing,* University of Nebraska Press 43-59. Lincoln, Nebraska.

Hathcock, Roy
1983   *The Quapaw and Their Pottery.* Hurley Press, Inc. Camden, Arkansas.

1988   *Ancient Indian Pottery of the Mississippi River.* Valley Walsworth Publishing Co. Marceline, Missouri.

Haury, Emil W.
1978   *The Hohokam, Desert Farmers and Craftsmen. Excavations at Snaketown, 1964-1965.* University of Arizona Press. Tucson, Arizona.

Hayden, Julian D.
1972   *Hohokam Petroglyphs of the Sierra Pinacate, Sonora, and the Hohokam Shell Expeditions. The Kiva* 37;74-83.

Heizer, R.
1974   *The World of the American Indian.* Washington, D.C.: The National Geographic Society.

Hill, James N.
1970   *Broken K Pueblo: prehistoric social organization in the American Southwest.* Anthropological Papers of the University of Arizona 18. Tucson, Arizona.

Hodge, Fredrick W.
1907-10

Handbook of American Indians North of Mexico. Part I. Rowman and Littlefield. Reprinted 1979 from the Thirtieth Annual Report of the Bureau of American Ethnology. Washington, D.C.

Holden, E. S.
1879-80

Studies in Central American Picture Writing. First Annual Report of the Bureau of American Ethnology. Washington, D.C.

Holmes, W. H.
1882-83

Pottery of the Ancient Pueblos. Fourth Annual Report to the Bureau of American Ethnology. Washington, D.C.

James, George Wharton
1974   *Indian Blankets and Their Makers, The Navajo.* The Rio Grande Press Inc. Glorieta, New Mexico.

James, H. L.
1988   *Rugs and Posts.* Schiffer Publishing Ltd. West Chester, Pennsylvania.

Kabotie, Fred
1949   *Designs from the Ancient Mimbrenos with a Hopi Interpretation.*   Grabhorn Press. San Francisco, California.

Kearns, Timothy M.
1973   *Abiotic Resources,* in *An Archaeological Survey of the Orme Reservoir,* assembled by Veletta Canouts and Mark Gready. Manuscript prepared for the U.S. Bureau of Reclamation, Central Arizona Project, on file at Arizona State Museum, University of Arizona. Tucson, Arizona.

Keightley, David N.
1989   *The Origins of Writing in China: Scripts and Cultural Contexts.* The Origins of Writing. The University of Nebraska Press 171-203. Lincoln, Nebraska.

Kidder, Alfred Vincent
1932   *The Artifacts of Pecos,* Papers of the Southwestern Expedition, no. 6, Phillips Academy. New Haven, Connecticut. (Yale University Press.)

Lang, Richard W.
1976   *An Archaeological Survey of the Upper San Cristobal Arroyo Drainage, in the Galiseo Basin, Santa Fe County, New Mexico.* School of American Research. Santa Fe, New Mexico.

LeBlanc, Steven A.
1983   *The Mimbres People: Ancient Pueblo Painters of the American Southwest.* Thames and Hudson Inc., New York, New York.

Lehmann, Ruth P. M.
1989   *Ogham: The Ancient Script of the Celts. The Origins of Writing.* The University of Nebraska Press 159-171. Lincoln, Nebraska.

Lister, Robert H. and Florence C. Lister
1987   *Aztec Ruins, on the Animas, Excavated, Preserved, and Interpreted.* University of New Mexico Press. Albuquerque, New Mexico.

Lounsbury, Floyd G.
1989   *The Ancient Writing of Middle America. The Origins of Writing.* The University of Nebraska Press 203-239. Lincoln, Nebraska.

Mails, Thomas E.
1983   *The Pueblo Children of the Mother Earth.* Vol. 1. Doubleday and Company, Inc.   Garden City, New York.

Mallery, Garrick
1879-1880

   Sign Language Among the North American Indians. First Annual Report to the Bureau of American Ethnology. Washington, D.C.

1882-1883

   Pictographs of the North American Indians. Fourth Annual Report of the Bureau of American Ethnology. Washington, D.C.

1888-1889

   Picture Writing of the American Indians. Tenth Annual Report of the Bureau of American Ethnology. Washington, D.C.

Martineau, LaVan
1987   *The Rocks Begin To Speak.* KC Publications. Las Vegas, Nevada.

Moulard, Barbara L.
1984   *Within the Underworld Sky. Mimbres Ceramic Art in Context.* Twelvetrees Press. Pasadena, California.

Mountjoy, Joseph B.
1974a *Some Hypotheses regarding the Petroglyphs of West Mexico,* Meso-American Studies No. 9, University Museum, Southern Illinois University. Carbondale, Illinois.

Mullet, G. M.
1979   *Spider Woman Stories, Legends of the Hopi Indians.* University of Arizona Press. Tucson, Arizona.

Needham, Rodney
1979   *Symbolic Classification.* Goodyear Publishing Company, Inc. Santa Monica, California.

Newcomb, F.J. and G. A. Reichard
1975   *Sandpaintings of the Navajo Shooting Chant.* Dover Publications, Inc. New York, New York.

Patterson, Alex
1992   *A Field Guide to Rock Art Symbols of the Greater Southwest.* Johnson Books. Boulder, Colorado.

Peckham, Stewart
1990   *From This Earth.* Museum of New Mexico Press. Santa Fe, New Mexico.

Pike, Donald G. and David Muench
1974   *Anasazi, Ancient People of the Rock.* Crown Publishers Inc. New York, New York.

Plog, Stephen.
1980   *Stylistic Variation in Prehistoric Ceramics. Design Analysis in the American Southwest.* Cambridge University Press. Cambridge, Massachusetts.

Reichard, Gladys A.
1950   *Navajo Religion: A Study of Symbolism,* vols. 1 and 2, Bollingen Series 18. Stanford Press. New York , New York.

1977   *Navajo Medicine Man Sandpaintings.* Dover Publications, Inc. New York, New York.

Robbins, R.R. and R. B. Westmoreland
1991   *Astronomical Imagery and Numbers in Mimbres Pottery.*

Rodee, Marian E.
1981   *Old Navajo Rugs, Their Development From 1900-1940.* University of New Mexico Press. Albuquerque, New Mexico.

1987   *Weaving of the Southwest.* Maxwell Museum of Anthropology, University of New Mexico. Schiffer Publishing Ltd. West Chester, Pennsylvania.

Schaafsma, Polly and Curtis F. Schaafsma
1974   *Evidence for the Origins of Pueblo Kachina Cult as Suggested by Southwestern Rock Art.* American Antiquity 39(4):535-545.

Schaafsma, Polly.
1980   *Indian Rock Art of the Southwest.* School of American Research. Southwest Indian Arts Series. University of New Mexico Press. Albuquerque, New Mexico.

Schele, L.
1977   *Palenque: the House of the Dying Sun. Native American Astronomy,* University of Texas Press. Austin, Texas.

Schmandt-Besserat
1989   *Two Precursors of Writing: Plain and Complex Tokens. The Origins of Writing.* University of Nebraska Press, 27-43. Lincoln, Nebraska.

Schmidt, Karl P. and Robert F. Inger
1975   *Living Reptiles of the World,* Doubleday Co. Inc. New York, New York.

1956 *Ceramics for the Archaeologist.* Carnegie Institution of Washington Pub. 609. Washington, D.C.

Seaman, N. G.
1967 *Indian Relics of the Pacific Northwest.* 2nd ed, Binfords and Mort. Portland, Oregon.

Senner, Wayne M.
1989 *Theories and Myths on the Origins of Writing: A Historical Overview. The Origins of Writing,* University of Nebraska Press. 1-27. Lincoln, Nebraska.

Shepard, A. O.
1942 *Rio Grande Glaze Paint Ware: A Study Illustrating the Place of Ceramic Technological Analysis in Archaeological Research.* Carnegie Inst. of Washington, Pub. 528, pp. 129-260. Washington, D.C.

Smith, Watson
1966 *The Excavation of Hawikuh, Report of the Hendricks-Hodge Expedition 1917-1923.* Museum of the American Indian, Heye Foundation. New York, NY.

Steen, Charlie R.
1966 *Excavations at Tse Ta'a, Canyon de Chelly National Monument,* Arizona. Archaeological Research Series no. 9, National Park Service. Washington, D.C.

Sternberg, Martin L. A.
1987 *American Sign Language Dictionary.* Harper and Row. New York, New York.

Stroud, Ronald S.
1989 *The Art of Writing in Ancient Greece. The Origins of Writing.* University of Nebraska Press 103-121. Lincoln, Nebraska.

Sturtevant, William C.
1979 *Handbook of North American Indians, Southwest.* Vol 9. Smithsonian Institution. Washington, D.C.

Thompson, J. S. E.
1967 *Creation Myths* (part 2). Estudios de Cultura Maya. Vol. 5. UNAM. Mexico City, Mexico

Turner, Christy G.
1963 *Petrographs of the Glen Canyon Region,* Museum of Northern Arizona Bulletin no. 38 (Glen Canyon Series no. 4). Flagstaff, Arizona.

Voth, H. R.
1905 *The Traditions of the Hopi,* Field Columbian Museum Publication 96, Anthropological Series vol. 8 Chicago, Illinois.

Wallace, Rex
1989 *The Origins and Development of the Latin Alphabet. The Origins of Writing.* University of Nebraska Press 121-137. Lincoln, Nebraska.

Walters, Frank
1977 *Book of the Hopi.* Penguin Books USA Inc. New York, New York.

Wellmann, K.F.
1975 *Some Observations on the Bird Motif in North American Indian Rock Art.* Paper presented at the symposium on American Indian Rock Art. El Paso, Texas.

Wendorf, Fred and Erik K. Reed
1955 *An Alternative Reconstruction of Northern Rio Grande Prehistory.* El Palacio 62:131-73.

Whitehead, Alfred North
1927 *Symbolism: Its Meaning and Effect.* Cambridge University Press. Cambridge, Massachusetts.

Wilson, Thomas
1894 *The Swastika.* Smithsonian Report, U.S. National Museum.

Wissler, Clark
1966 *Indians of the United States.* Doubleday and Co. Inc. Garden City, New York.

Woodbury, Richard B. and Nathalie F.S. Woodbury
1966 *Decorated Pottery of the Zuni Area.* Appendix II. In, *Contributions From the Museum of the American Indian,* Heye Foundation, Vol. XX. Watson Smith. New York, New York.

Wright, Barton
1973 *Kachinas, a Hopi Artist's Documentary.* Northland Press, Flagstaff, Arizona with the Heard Museum. Phoenix, Arizona.

1985 *Kachinas of the Zuni.* Northland Press. Flagstaff, Arizona.

Wu, Hung
1985 *Bird Motifs in Eastern Yi Art.* Orientations 16.10 (Oct. 85) 34-36, figures 9,10,11,13,15,17. China Books, San Francisco, CA

Yarrow, H. C.
1879-80
A Study of Mortuary Customs of the North American Indians. First Annual Report to the Bureau of American Ethnology. Washington, D.C.

Zubrow, Ezra B. W.
1972 *Carrying Capacity and Dynamic Equilibrium in the Prehistoric Southwest.* In *Contemporary Archaeology.* Edited by Mark P. Leone, pp. 268-279. Southern Illinois University Press. Carbondale, Illinois.

Index to Photographs

Index to Figures

INDEX

About the Author

Since a boy on exploring adventures with his father, James Cunkle traveled into remote areas of the Southwest and discovered the West's unspoiled natural beauty. These impressions remained with James throughout his life, haunting him into adulthood.

When James was in his early teens, he would leave the East the day that school ended in June and hitchhike to the West. With a bedroll under one arm, and a suitcase swinging at his side, he crossed hundreds of miles of wilderness and discovered prehistoric caves, petroglyphs, and archaeological sites that were unrecorded.

He entered Eastern Michigan University in Ypsilanti in 1969 and completed two years of academia. Cunkle's studies focused him toward a career in teaching.

In 1971, Cunkle left Eastern Michigan and became an artist for the next ten years. He created sculptures of glass and bronze.

Adventure called and Cunkle traveled to the headwaters of the Amazon River in Columbia, where he and a team of entomologists collected insects using a portable generator and ultraviolet lights.

Cunkle became a pilot. He soloed in less than eight hours, and built and flew experimental aircraft.

He became a scuba diver, sky diver, cave spelunker, and he learned to sail.

In the 1980s, James traveled to the Yucatan jungles of Mexico to record the vanishing life ways of the Maya Indians. Also during this adventure, the team explored the depths of Mayan caves and cenotes using scuba gear and metal detectors.

Cunkle dreamed of making a personal contribution to the sciences and the study of humankind.

Toward that end, in 1988 he graduated Cum Laude and received a B.A. in Anthropology/Archaeology from Cleveland State University, Cleveland, Ohio.

Continued next page . . .

(About the Author continued)

During his undergraduate career, James and his colleagues published two scientific papers: ***Distal Radius and Proximal Femur Fracture Patterns in the Hamann-Todd Skeletal Collection*** and ***An Unknown Burial Site on Kelly's Island***. The distal radius fracture study was one of the first reports to recognize the correlation between supplemental estrogen, vitamin D and calcium in older women, in order to decrease osteoporosis.

Cunkle and his colleagues are currently working on Raven Site Ruin in northeastern Arizona at the base of the White Mountains, twelve miles north of Springerville. The site has provided the majority of the data which encompass this work.

The Raven Site, known to have had several occupations over the past 800 years, was secured by the White Mountain Archaeological Center after having been at the mercy of pots hunters.

As Coordinator and Director of Research, Cunkle, along with his wife Carol, operate the Center, a facility open to the general public and devoted to preserving, protecting and discovering the past through education and a hands-on exposure to field archaeology.

Also by James R. Cunkle

TREASURES OF TIME

A Guide to Prehistoric Ceramics of the Southwest

A user-friendly guide to the ceramics that have been unearthed at Raven Site Ruins in northeastern Arizona. Author/archaeologist James R. Cunkle categorizes the primary groups of prehistoric ceramics found at the site and treats each in a separate chapter of in-depth information. Includes full-color insert, glossary and index.

6 x 9 — 216 Pages . . . $14.95

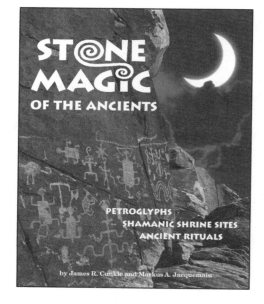

STONE MAGIC OF THE ANCIENTS

A Guide to Petroglyphs of the Southwest

Discover prehistoric shrine sites and explore the ritual uses of rock imagery. Authors James R. Cunkle and Markus A. Jacquemain provide a detailed presentation of Southwestern petroglyphs. Filled with hundreds of previously unpublished photographs and illustrations, *Stone Magic of the Ancients* presents evidence of the unique spiritual connection prehistoric shamans placed on their rock image creations. Images presented include Kokopelli, anthropomorphs and zoomorphs.

8 x 10 — 192 Pages . . . $14.95

More Great Books from Golden West Publishers!

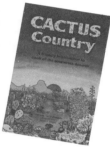

ORDER BLANK

GOLDEN WEST PUBLISHERS

4113 N. Longview Ave
Phoenix, AZ 85014

Number of Copies	TITLE	Per Copy	AMOUNT
	Arizona Adventure	6.95	
	Arizona Cook Book	5.95	
	Arizona Crosswords	4.95	
	Arizona Legends and Lore	6.95	
	Arizona Museums	9.95	
	Arizona—Off the Beaten Path	6.95	
	Arizona Outdoor Guide	6.95	
	Cactus Country	6.95	
	Discover Arizona!	6.95	
	Explore Arizona!	6.95	
	Fishing Arizona	7.95	
	Ghost Towns in Arizona	6.95	
	Hiking Arizona	6.95	
	Horse Trails in Arizona	9.95	
	In Old Arizona	6.95	
	Old West Adventures in Arizona	6.95	
	Prehistoric Arizona	5.00	
	Quest for the Dutchman's Gold	6.95	
	Scorpions & Venomous Insects/SW	9.95	
	Snakes and Other Reptiles of the SW	9.95	
	Stone Magic of the Ancients	14.95	
	Tales of Arizona Territory	6.95	
	Talking Pots	19.95	
	Treasures of Time	14.95	
	Verde River Recreation Guide	6.95	
	Wild West Characters	6.95	
Shipping & Handling		+ $2.00	

☐ My Check or Money Order Enclosed. . . . . $ _____
☐ MasterCard   ☐ VISA   (Payable in U.S. funds)

Acct. No. _____ Exp. Date _____

Signature _____

Name _____ Phone _____

Address _____

City/State/Zip _____

Talking Pots

Golden West's specialty is the Southwest!

- Characters and legends of the Wild West!

- Prospecting, hiking, fishing, horseback riding, motorcycling and more!

- Learn to cook Southwestern style! Over 40 cook books to choose from!

- Wildlife posters!

- Western music and story tapes!

- Children's activity books. Learn about Southwestern states, Indians, National Monuments!

Order your FREE Golden West Publishers Catalog

1-800-658-5830 or 602-265-4392
FAX 602-279-6901

GOLDEN WEST ☼ PUBLISHERS